FRED KLEISER

630 319
    /431

The
Millennial
CEO

- Fred -

Thanks for being
a source of inspiration
for Stacy! You like entrepreneurial
She says, you
thinking!
She is one of the Best!

The Millennial CEO

© 2012 By

Daniel Newman

ALL RIGHTS RESERVED

Cover art design by Christina Isabel Gray

ISBN: 978-0-9854148-9-4

First Printing: 2012

MARIE STREET PRESS

5930 Royal Lane Suite E-373 Dallas, TX 75230

Tel +1 214.519.8033

http://millennialceo.com

http://mariestreetpress.com

ADVANCE PRAISE FOR
THE MILLENNIAL CEO

"Millennials seem terminally trapped between the desire to lead... and the opportunity to lead. Daniel serves as a role model on how best to cross the leadership chasm – and make a difference based on your ability to lead and motivate, rather than your birth generation."– *Mark Babbitt, CEO and Founder, YouTern.com*

"While this book is written for, well, Millennials, the advice on leadership and operations is valuable for anyone running a business. I recommend all business leaders of all ages read this book. You will learn not only how to adapt to adversity and change, but how to embrace several generations in the workplace." – *Gini Dietrich, CEO, Arment Dietrich, Inc. Author of* Spin Sucks *and co-author of* Marketing in the Round

"The world has changed so dramatically in the last few years and businesses are struggling to keep up. The successful, social businesses of the future will be led by open and transparent leaders. If you are looking for a great story on how to win in today's competitive environment with effective leadership skills, you should read this book." – *Michael Brenner, Content Strategist for SAP and author of the* B2B Marketing Insider, *co-founder of Business2Community.com*

"A wonderful and insightful read for aspiring and current leaders who understand that there is no safety in the status quo. As a proven innovative leader, with a sustained track record of success, Daniel's thought leadership will inspire you to drive change and fuel both personal and professional growth."
– *Vala Afshar – CMO and Chief Customer Officer, Enterasys Networks (Twitter: @ValaAfshar)*

"If you're a millennial CEO, or plan to be one, you must read this book! It's full of wisdom, humanity, insight and transparency into the business-building process for the social media set. Read it now!" – *Christine Comaford, CEO Advisor, NY Times Bestselling Author, www.ChristineComaford.com*

"Two things about Daniel Newman: 1. In my work with executives I quote him a lot – due to the impact of his insights, there's usually a silent 'Wow!' 2. I know senior executives who openly embrace generational reverse-mentoring to catch up on social media - they actually need to reverse mentor with Dan for his millennial leadership skills."– *Alan Kay, Solutions leadership for many organizations. www.alankay.ca*

"As a Millennial, and a CEO who interacts with corporate CEOs of all generations, Dan's background and writings really hit home. The nuance of a Millennial voice, backed with tangible experience and credentials provides a look at the do's and don'ts for leadership, success and tenacity that is required of any great leader to succeed – regardless of their generation. Read the book, internalize and practice Dan's teachings, then share the message with your colleagues, friends and others you meet on the road to success!" – *Ben Smithee, Chief Executive Officer of Spych Market Analytics*

"What sets this book apart is Dan's unique perspective. Not only is he a CEO, but he's also a college professor, and a co-founder 12most.com – one of the fastest-growing blogs on the internet. As an instructor, entrepreneur and leader, Dan knows what it takes to create success. Read this book, and find out how to reach your true potential." – *Ted Coine, Author, Speaker, Co-founder of the Switch and Shift blog (http://switchandshift.com)*

Most generations don't think about leadership until the last generation retires and moves on. But one Millennial was cast into the role at a very young age, and as such, has to take the lead on thinking about leadership and leading his generation. Dan's book will help you think about how to successfully lead the next generation. Scratch that. Dan's book will help you think about leading successfully. Period. – *S. Anthony Iannarino,   President, Solutions Staffing and Adjunct Faculty, Capital University http://www.thesalesblog.com*

"Here's a unique perspective and guide for Gen Y – and others – who want to create a better future for themselves. Read this book, and find out what you need to know about yourself, your team and your potential! Highly recommended." - *Angela Maiers, Speaker, Writer, Passionate Educator*

TABLE OF CONTENTS

OXFORD comma

FOREWORD BY CHRIS WESTFALL

Why does everyone pick on Millennials?

From books, we learn that "Not Everyone Gets a Trophy". Tales of the tech-savvy and entitled are commonplace these days. But, are these stories true?

In my experience, a pundit's perspective is never the whole story. And if you've picked up this title, I suspect that you are not interested in stereotypes or research, but a real-life chronicle of ups and downs, with some guidance along the way.

In my book, *The NEW Elevator Pitch*, I talked a lot about the importance of a person's story. More specifically, the ability to tell your story in a way that's persuasive, concise and compelling. For example, a story about someone defying the odds. A story about overcoming stereotypes; a story about how to create something unexpected.

For me, that's the story of *The Millennial CEO*. I've been friends with Daniel Newman for quite a while. When we first met, he was a sales representative in Chicago. Coming from the Chicago suburbs, we had a common background – but I knew right away that Dan was an uncommon guy.

We worked together on a couple of projects – projects that created career opportunities for both of us – and I watched his story unfold.

Like all good stories, there were challenges and adversity. (There are more adjectives to describe the place where we used to work, but I'll stop with those two).

However, the best stories don't get stuck on what's wrong – they concentrate on making it right.

When I sat down to write the chapter on how to use *The NEW Elevator Pitch* to move your career forward, I wanted to connect with someone who had to walk the walk, as opposed to studying the walk, taking a sabbatical to ponder the walk, and then lecturing about the walk that others had taken. I featured Daniel Newman's career experience as a resource in my book, because it was his experience that really intrigued me.

Think about it: experience is something we all have. Some of us have more than others. Some have experience in areas that are highly valuable; some experiences seem relatively meaningless, particularly in a corporate or business context. But no matter where you are in your career, your experience is both an asset, and a liability – depending on how you make it relevant.

How can you take your experience and turn it into something meaningful for the people that matter most to you? In essence, that question is the central theme of my book. Understand how to make your experience matter, and you can influence the way that you manage your career, your customers, your employees and your relationships. Making your experience relevant and valuable is really the trick – it's not necessarily about the amount of experience. The value comes when you can use your past history to create a new and more compelling future.

I'm passionate about helping Millennials to tell their story, and that theme was really the driving force behind my grand-prize winning elevator pitch. (Check it out on my YouTube channel if you're curious). My remarks centered on proving the value of the college degree – a question that faces every Millennial at some point or another. It's part of a larger question that goes beyond your birthdate and education, namely: what's your unique value proposition? What's the "special sauce" that you have to offer?

Your story is about more than your experiences or academic studies – it's about what you can do for others. Daniel Newman is someone who discovered how to create a value equation that went beyond his experience. Here's his roadmap - with the bumps and bruises along the way - for your consideration.

Why not get serious about making your experience matter to others, and see what happens in your career, your causes and your relationships? Get ready for the rest of the story from the guy who's lived it – the story of *The Millennial CEO*.

– Chris Westfall

SECTION I:

LEADERSHIP

MOMENTS IN TIME

Tweet This:

If the secret of success is all in the timing, then maybe the time to start something must be…right now!

When I was 21 years old, life was staring at me and I couldn't even blink. Uncertainty was everywhere. I had no idea what was ahead of me. Taking on marriage, fatherhood and trying to figure out "what I wanted to be when I grew up" was a lot to take on all at one time. Can you relate?

Knowing the next move is always a mystery, and life seems to provide endless complications. We are all surrounded by economic complications, personal complications and professional complications. Nevertheless, there was a choice to be made. No matter where you are in your life, your path is always yours to decide.

When I realized that I had the opportunity to make some changes, I saw a set of actions that propelled me forward on my journey. These defining moments are what led me to write this book, and share my experiences with you.

Perhaps my journey can help you with yours.

Perhaps my story can help you to understand others and understand some of the generational differences that we all need to recognize.

I think it is important for you the reader to understand a little bit about the format of this book. In today's world of information overload, this book is designed in a way where it can be consumed in byte-sized (pun intended) portions. While the stories and lessons that comprise the chapters in this book certainly build off of one another, they also stand alone. So, you can enjoy this book in a sitting or over the course of several weeks.

At the ripe old age of 21, the stakes were high – but my determination was higher. I was determined to rise above my circumstances – circumstances that may not be that different from the challenges that you are facing today.

While I can't say that I had a clear path, I had a clear decision. In order to change my situation, I had to decide to move past the status quo. But towards what, exactly?

There was a time when I looked at the pieces of my life, and stopped asking "Why me?" I realized that looking outwardly at external factors – like the state of the economy, or slow data rates (What are slow data rates?), or even my own personal missteps – was all part of the same mistake.

I had to focus on the things I could control and change what I could for the sake of my family and my future.

It may sound silly or immature (I'll leave other adjectives to you to decide), but I consciously committed to move forward with a relentless pursuit of "greatness." While we each define greatness differently, the bottom line is all of us desire to achieve it. Just starting my twenties, I don't know if I had a clear definition of "greatness" – but I knew I needed to move forward and turn my situation around. Today, I'm still finding out what "greatness" means, and I'm not sure if I'll ever reach it. But, the greatest thing that I can share with you is the way I have made changes along my journey.

That's really what this book is about: sharing my experiences in a way that can make your journey more productive and rewarding. My hope is that my observations and insights, whatever they may be, will help you tap into your own personal leadership skills. I believe that greatness is a worthwhile pursuit, and something that lives within all of us. Do you?

The journey to greatness is worth getting excited about. It's been my experience that this journey is as much an internal one as a pursuit of a destination or goal. Leadership can happen at any level, and leadership skills exist outside of titles and roles. So keep your eyes on the road ahead - because your defining moments are out there just waiting to be realized.

WHY THE PAST MATTERS

It is often said that the past is just that, "The Past" and there is no point in looking back.

I don't think there is a saying that could be more wrong.

The past is like a vault full of riches and knowledge – a treasure trove that we can all learn so much from. Greatness comes to those who learn from the past and create a future that's based on a fresh perspective.

One of the signposts on the journey ahead, attributed to Albert Einstein: "He who has never failed, has probably never attempted to do much."

It is in our many attempts to accomplish many things that we will succeed. But success is hardly guaranteed.

Failure is where you will find your compass. My failures are the source of my success. And coping with the inevitable disappointment is the way you will define your career, and your character.

I believe that failure isn't truly a failure, if you learn from it and take action – you've got to keep moving forward. Failure itself was a lesson that helps you make the next attempt a success.

> *"A man can fail many times, but he isn't a failure until he begins to blame somebody else."*
> *– John Burroughs, American conservationist*

You must always drive forward in your career, but you cannot and should not ever blatantly ignore the past. You cannot deny the expertise of other generations. You cannot deny your own expertise, and your own intuition. Within the

5

moments of great instruction; in the future you will
ᴢ the fruits of your learning.

This Book Is About Y-O-U

So enough about me. What I really want to talk about is
you!

If you are a Millennial (like me) then chances are your
story is just beginning. No matter where you are in your life
or your career, there are still chapters left to be written.

New beginnings – and new perspectives – are not
generation-specific. Understanding how to manage and lead
across generations is a skill that we all need to learn.

So this isn't a book about Millennials, really. It's about a
Millennial perspective – in fact, a Millennial CEO
perspective – but you got that from the title. My story is
about someone who has worked with all the generations
before him, and plans to work with every generation after.
Why? Because effective collaboration is the key to
greatness.

Regardless of where you are in life, the choice to be great
is your own. And remember, that age is a state of mind. If
you are an ineffective jerk, that probably has more to do
with your personality than the date on your birth certificate.
Wouldn't you agree?

Ultimately, this book is about personal effectiveness. Can
you get things done when you need to? Can you inspire

others when you need them? Can you harness technology when your business demands it?

You can be certain that your impact will be determined by how well you can influence others. Influence is the centerpiece of leadership. Influence is what many Millennials lack; but this belief needs a makeover. The leaders of tomorrow are those who understand the secrets of influence.

While the stories that inspired much of the content here may be based on my experiences, these lessons in leadership, social media and personal effectiveness are universal. Look inside your organization – in fact, look into every organization with a heartbeat – and you will find a need for leadership. What's your story when it's time for you to lead?

I believe that your success in business (and in life) will be dependent on three things:

1. **Leadership**

2. **Social IQ** – are you savvy in the ways of social media? How about just plain ol' social skills, in real life?

3. **Operations** – are you effective when it comes time to "get it done"?

These three subjects comprise the main sections of this book.

Leadership: At the very highest level your journey will start and stop as fast as you can lead. Leadership is more than just how you motivate others, but your entire approach to human interaction. No matter how much you believe that you can do something on your own, you cannot. We need each other, and you need others to accelerate your journey. The ability to influence those whose life you touch will directly affect your ability to accomplish anything you aspire to achieve. So, how do you make the connections that matter?

Social and Technology: The world is quickly getting smaller because of the rapid proliferation of technology. The ability to connect with just about anyone on earth is now at our fingertips – changing the way we work, interact and live our lives. Technology has leveled the playing field, and made every industry smaller. Your ability to reach your target audience has become easier, but not necessarily simpler. You have the opportunity to embrace technology and use it as a spring board to your success. However: you must be cautious! We are all more exposed than ever as technology brings our connections closer than ever – sometimes, even too close for comfort!

Operations: The application of your leadership and your social influence to drive the results that matter. Throughout my career, I have seen that a strategy is only as good as its execution. You've got to operate within a context of leadership and social awareness, but apply those skills in a way that creates results. This section of the book will share some of the more difficult lessons I have learned, as I've applied (and attempted to apply!) my most significant strategies.

Throughout the book we will explore how these cross-generational topics can influence your journey, and lead you toward your own personal greatness.

As you navigate through the book, I challenge you to put yourself in my shoes. Why couldn't you be the Millennial CEO? And, if you are from a different generation, don't let your birthday keep you from being effective with everyone you influence. Today is the perfect day to start being more productive, and more deliberate in your pursuit of greatness.

Think about how you would handle a situation I bring up or how you may be able to apply a lesson that I perhaps had to learn the hard way. While the knowledge that I have gained through experience may make up the words on the page, it is your application that will resonate as you continue to create your story.

A YOUNG CEO'S JOURNEY
THE EVENTS... THE LESSONS

Tweet This:

Everyone has moments that define their very being. What are yours?

As I reflect on the journey to CEO at a spry 29 years of age, I was able to point to five critical events that shaped my path and made me the person I am today. I would like to share these events with you, as they have been such important moments in my journey.

EVENT #1: THE SURPRISE OF A LIFETIME

When I was 19 years old and a sophomore at Truman State University, I enjoyed participating on the men's soccer team, attending functions for my fraternity, and occasionally I even studied.

Late in my sophomore year, I was informed by my wife (then girlfriend) that we were going to be parents. She was a senior at that time, and I remember the moment like it was yesterday.

For a split second time stood still. It was upon returning from a weekend soccer tournament. She came over almost immediately upon my return and basically just dropped the news.

This moment was life-changing for me; it was in that instant that I had to decide whether or not to quickly grow up and become a father and a man, or to walk away from the situation like so many others do.

The Lesson: In all of our paths towards whatever we deem to be success, we are going to have to hurdle adversity. This situation, for me, was the first major adversity I had to face. And the decision would last a life time. Obviously the decision I made was to take on the responsibility, and I can proudly say it may be the best decision that I ever made. *Keyword: Adversity*

EVENT #2: THE PATH OF LEAST RESISTANCE

My father was a lifetime entrepreneur. He built his business without a college education and much parental support to speak of. He built a successful trucking company in Chicago. When I was finishing college (as a father and husband) I wasn't exactly sure what the career road map was going to be. As many in a family business do, I worked for my father because it provided two things I needed at the time: a job and money. While still in school, finding a career seemed daunting and difficult.

After a few years the discussion started arising about me taking over the business. I was told I would have to learn trucking from the ground up, but it could someday be mine. After some thought, I came to the conclusion that I didn't have any passion for the trucking business whatsoever, and regardless of the great financial opportunity it may provide me, it wasn't for me.

A mere 18 months later, my father sold the business and the decision became permanent.

The Lesson: While I do not subscribe to the "You can be anything" mentality, I do believe that real success is founded in doing something you are passionate about. I knew I wasn't passionate about the trucking business and the decision to take another route provided different challenges. By entering an industry (technology) that I was passionate about, my career has proven much more fulfilling. *Keyword: Passion*

EVENT #3: HOW THEY HUMBLE YE

In 2006 I was leading Midwest sales for a successful technology company by the name of AMX. I was the first direct hire in the territory and I was driving about 16 million dollars in sales. This territory had long been stagnant, not seeing meaningful growth in years, and I was set on getting it done. A compensation plan had been drawn up with a target growth of 20%. If I hit that target, both the company and I would be elated.

That year we worked tirelessly to grow our business. We cultivated new customers and brought back to life old ones. It was on the 364th day of the year that the final order needed to hit the 20% growth came in. I was so pleased with the entire team, and even more so with myself. At 25 years old, I had accomplished what so many others in the past hadn't – and I was paid handsomely to do so.

The next year, the VP of Sales came out with a new comp plan where I wouldn't be able to earn even half of what I had the year before. Outraged by this, I took the issue all the way to the top. I was convinced that this was a raw deal and that I should get special consideration given my success for the company. I ultimately sat down with the CEO to discuss my options.

He told me, "This is the deal. And there is the door if you don't like it".

The Lesson: To this day, I do not have much respect for the way the situation was handled. However, the event taught me about humility. I genuinely believed that I was above the law, better than the rest, and deserved special treatment. Looking back, I am surprised I could fit my head through the door. Being humble has paid dividends many times over since then, and it will always be a key to the success I have and will achieve. *Keyword: Humility*

EVENT #4: HIGHER LEARNING

One afternoon late in 2007 I received a letter from North Central College about attending an MBA open house. I had been vacillating around the idea of pursuing a master's degree. It wasn't long ago that a senior executive critically said that my lack of an MBA was holding me back.

While I didn't really care what others had to say, I have long been a fan of what Stephen Covey calls "Sharpening the Sword": the process of continuing to invest in oneself to reach higher levels of understanding.

Moreover, I knew that I wanted to make a run for the top, and that the continued education would prove valuable.

I opened the letter from North Central. I looked at my wife and said, "Honey, I'm going to get my MBA this year."

I remember she looked up and said, "Okay."

She later told me, it was that day that she knew I was going to do it. The program was a one year executive MBA, and it was an intense 50 week regimen. I was traveling 3 days a week for work and I was forced to schedule my travel and my life around school. The work was rigorous, and free time was non-existent. However, one year later, I received my Masters in Business, and that can never be taken away from me.

The Lesson: I often minimize the value of the MBA, or any degree for that matter. Mostly because if you lack the intangibles of being a good human, the education just doesn't amount to much. However, the story of pursuing and completing my MBA is a tale of persistence, commitment, and tenacity.

Like so many things in life, you have to make a decision about what is important to you. If education matters to you, you need to commit to the goal and achieve it at almost any cost. This approach translates to so many things, but earning an MBA made me realize that I can accomplish just about anything if I want it bad enough. *Keyword: Commitment*

EVENT #5: CHANGE IS POSSIBLE

It's a little known fact that I spent a little over a year around 2003 working for a Chicago-based technology integrator. I served in a Regional Sales role, overseeing higher education and health care. During my time there, I was successful, but I was also very young, and the humility I mentioned previously had not yet caught up with me. One of the owners at the time (Bob) was responsible for the company's service department.

For whatever reason, Bob and I got off on the wrong foot. During my time there, we never did find common ground. Upon my leaving, it was for quite some time that Bob and some others within the organization saw me as a problem child. From their viewpoint, I had left quite a few fires behind me as I left the organization. Our mutual perception of one another was pretty negative; however, over the next several years we had to work together because I was a vendor to my previous company.

Due to the continued relationship, forced or not, Bob and I started a dialogue. Over time, we began to better understand one another. It was still a surprise when I received a call from Bob early in 2009 asking if I would be interested in leading the company's sales and business development strategy. Hesitantly, I agreed to talk. We met for lunch, and we had an amazing conversation. From VP of Sales to Operations Executive to CEO in just a few short years. That's how the story started, when I turned a challenging relationship into a lifetime opportunity.

The Lesson: Change is incredibly hard; I have seen that in every facet of my life. Having said that, change is possible. People who resist change or fail to recognize it will miss out on many of life's great opportunities. The fact that I am a CEO is 100% based upon a mutual willingness to recognize and embrace change. Bob and I could have decided almost a decade ago that we would never work together again. Today, we have a great professional relationship that has been built in trust, communication, and a willingness to change. *Keyword: Change*

THE FUTURE

My crystal ball is the same as yours – I really have no exact idea of where this journey will take me. I do know that so much of what has been accomplished can be attributed to having a vision of what's to come, combined with an acute awareness of "The Now."

Life for me has provided great adversity as well as fulfillment, just as it has for so many others. The lessons I learned from those events have exponentially improved the quality of my life in so many areas.

TIME FOR A MILLENNIAL TO SPEAK FOR MILLENNIALS

Tweet This:

> *It's great when researchers take the time to generalize an entire generation. But it is better when we speak for ourselves.*

Over the past few months I have closely followed the crowd as they speak about the "Mysterious Millennial" as it relates to life, work, and social skills.

Article after article is riddled with opinions, stereotypes, and generalizations about an entire generation that does little more than magnify the shortcomings and belittle the contribution that the next generation brings to society.

What are these supposed shortcomings? Well, I've noted many in books and media – how about you? The general consensus seems to be made up of the following... I'll entitle them "The Myths"

Myth 1: We're Entitled – We believe that the world should be handed to us. For instance a college degree means we should be given a key to the executive office.

17

Myth 2: We're Self Centered – We don't see beyond ourselves. In short: Gen Y believes that the world revolves around us rather than the sun.

Myth 3: We're Lazy – We aren't willing to get our hands dirty. The boomers worked hard for their success and the Millennials think it should be ours, because we showed up.

Myth 4: We're Fragile – We can't take criticism. Further, we require constant ego stroking.

Myth 5: We're Never Leaving Home – We don't have the will or drive to go out on our own. If our parents allowed it, we would never move fly from the nest.

Well I've read and I've listened. Now, I have decided it is time to speak up, to enlighten on where this all comes from and then present the truth at least as it is seen in the eyes of this Millennial.

Ironically the content isn't coming from Millennials but rather from a rash of Gen X and Baby Boomers who are filling up the interwebs and making their living off of teaching, preaching, and misguiding business after business about the wants and needs of Millennials.

I suppose that opinions of all shapes and sizes are welcome to any debate, so I'm not suggesting that the older generations don't continue to write about the Millennial. I am however putting it out there that it is time for more Millennials to speak up about the contributions that we are making and how we are shaping the future.

If for nothing else than to refute the mass (inaccurate) communications that are being delivered on our behalf, someone has to set the record straight.

While some of the things that the experts say may be true within the constraints of the research, it's also true that Millennials are next. It is this misunderstood, overgeneralized generation that will lead the evolution, revolution, and transformation of our world.

And guess what, in some ways we already have! Mark Zuckerberg, a Millennial and Facebook founder, has forever transformed the way we communicate with our friends, family, and the world. With nearly 800 million users, Facebook has transcended every traditional media growth rate and is now the de facto standard communication platform for individuals and businesses alike. Other highly commercialized platforms such as Pinterest, FourSquare, and WordPress were all products of the Millennial.

A clear picture cannot be built on myths. The picture of the Millennial, created by research and Baby Boomers, is not a complete picture. When trying to define a generation, the clear picture must be built on truth, not myths. The clearest picture comes from the heart and mind of a Millennial. Here are my truths in relation to the previously identified myths.

MYTH 1: ENTITLED

Truth: We need to not confuse entitled with having big dreams. Millennials are very entrepreneurial and we desire to make a substantial contribution right away. Perhaps we are impatient, but we want to see more rapid change. Remember, we have lived through a technological revolution like none ever before. Fast is the only speed we know.

MYTH 2: SELF CENTERED

Truth: While perhaps progressive at times in our thinking, we see selflessness as a more global effort whereas generations before tended to pursuit this within family and community. While we may not have the same sense of family values and perhaps that is unfortunate, we have brought social good and consciousness to a whole new level (think of post-tsunami Japan). Think about the revolutions that we have helped facilitate around the world (Egypt) by utilizing our modern means of communication. Millennial adoption of technology is making the world that much smaller!

MYTH 3: LAZY

Truth: We aren't lazy (entirely); we think that there are different and more transformative ways to deal with problems. However, since most of us work for and with older generations, they still want to do things the old/hard way. What defines the "hard way" is a matter of perspective. This book is about a fresh perspective, and doing things differently.

Why?

Because there IS A BETTER WAY! All generations discuss productivity over perceived effort. The "hard way" is perceived effort. My way? Productivity. There's nothing lazy about it.

MYTH 4: WE'RE FRAGILE

Truth: I think the reality is we may be more expressive of our feelings. In the past being open and sensitive was taboo, now it isn't. From our early upbringing, we Millennials were pushed more to be expressive and to be sensitive beings. While this can present challenges in the workplace, it also enhances opportunities for real communication. While I am an advocate for sometimes limiting your personal feelings in the workplace, we weren't born to be miserable either.

MYTH 5: WE'RE NEVER LEAVING HOME

Truth: Many Millennials happened to come out of school during one of the worst economic times since the great depression (this economy may have been worse than 1929-1936 – as I write this, the jury's still out). There are many potential reasons for the lack of immediate success for Millennials: a tough job market, high cost of living, frozen credit markets, etc...

So I'm not sure that the data related to Millennials moving back home is as related to their desire to be there as it is their need for a roof.

I don't know a single Millennial that's ever said, "Wow, I would love to live at home." Necessity and desire are two different things.

So there you have it. Perhaps the truth is in the eyes of the Millennial, and not in the eyes of the data sample. This perspective means new ideas, a global viewpoint, a different type of work ethic, an open demeanor, and a desire to create our own success. (And move out of the house!)

LEADERSHIP: TITLE NOT REQUIRED

Tweet This:

Does the title on your business card dictate whether or not you are a leader?

For the longest time there has been a correlation between top managers, executives, and the act of leadership. While the expectation that people in high level positions should provide leadership, the actual act of leadership isn't always guaranteed by those who reside in the highest ranks. I attribute this action/expectation disconnect to the widely misunderstood fact that *leadership is not a position, it is an activity*. And while the buzz around being a leader continues to grow (with close parallels to politics and business), the only genuine way to be a leader is to lead.

The great thing about this simple observation is that unlike high-level management opportunities, which may be limited, leadership isn't an exclusive opportunity or abstract concept.

In fact, leading is something that almost anyone can do, any day of the week, from anywhere. First, before anything can be accomplished, one must realize the boundless opportunity for leadership. This realization is the key so that you can begin to focus on how to lead each day, rather than waiting to be put into a position to lead.

After all, in today's performance economy, sometimes you have to do the job to get the job.

So showing leadership even when it isn't expected may just make you a shoe-in for the next level.

Here are some ways you can lead, without title, while subsequently making your organization better.

- **Kill the mill** – People love to gossip. It has led to a multibillion-dollar industry known as the tabloids. The productivity-killing behavior of rumor-mongering isn't limited to celebrities. People love to spread company gossip around. Much like many of the tabloids, the information isn't always completely true (or true at all). When given the opportunity to carry on a rumor or squash it, the leader knows what to do.

- **Remember The Golden Rule** – It is so easy to get caught up in the finger pointing, name calling, and relative immaturity that can feast inside of an organization. People by nature can be very judgmental - and judgment rarely yields positive feelings or interaction. A continued focus on treating others kindly and avoiding the traps of judgment and deceit is a great way to be a leader.

- **Be Inclusive** – So many organizations become soiled with the likes of politics. Camps based on function, manager, division etc. are everywhere. These campouts are devastating to an organization, and divisiveness becomes perpetuated throughout the ranks. Whether inviting a few new employees to lunch or gathering the input of different team members into your projects, being inclusive tears down walls. Including multiple viewpoints is a simple way to lead day in and day out.

- **Push Your Peers** – When a manager has to push an employee, it is often seen as a contentious interaction. The employee often feels scolded, no matter how the news was delivered. This is more a byproduct of the manager/employee relationship than anything else. One thing that I love to see is when a teammate gives her teammate a swift kick in the rear. When a team member verbalizes in a highly professional way that they would like to see more from their teammate, it often drives improved behavior – rather than the feeling of inadequacy that can come from managerial discipline.

- **Lend a Hand** – Even if something isn't technically your responsibility, that doesn't mean you can't chip in. If you have know-how that can push an idea or a project forward, step up and reach out. While there is no certainty that your attempts will be appreciated, each one of us make contributions to the culture and this is a practice every company can benefit from.

Whether you hold the top post or you are feeding the boxes in the mailroom, leadership opportunities are everywhere. How do you lead everyday with or without a title?

THREE TRUTHS, A LIE, AND A LEADER

Tweet This:

Be careful not to make snap judgments. People, including you, are complex. Remember that!

About 10 years ago I had aspirations of being a world-renowned club DJ and producer. In fact, for about 2 years I was traveling all over North America, playing in clubs while producing records that can still be bought online today. As I was telling that story to a friend, I got a surprising reaction.

After hearing my story, my friend looked at me and said that sounds like "The Lie" from the game "Three Truths and a Lie". Do you know this game?

My friend was insinuating that there was no way that she could believe that I was the person I once was. Knowing me today, my past seemed too crazy for her to believe.

Crazy, because it most certainly was me. At that point I still had hair – and I'm not sure I knew what a CEO was.

This incident made me think a lot about many things. How can we change so much throughout the course of our lives? I began to wonder about the assumptions that we make, about the people we know. Perhaps more importantly: what we really don't know.

Do we too often assume we know too much?

When I went back to school to earn my MBA I had a leadership professor that used to say, "You think you see through others so well; what makes you think they can't see through you?"

A profound maxim that made me realize that leadership must be genuine, or chances are your "not so real ways" will soon be discovered – making leadership that much more difficult.

While profound indeed, this authenticity maxim has a flaw. It represents only what people see now. While now does reflect a still frame in time, it often neglects who we were... and who we will become.

One of the things that we rarely consider is that people in many ways are fluid. Life is in a state of constant change. As individuals, we make gradual change on a daily basis. The sum of those changes can make us nearly unrecognizable over a greater period of time.

In the analogy of "Three Truths and a Lie", the Lie serves as a metaphor for what we don't know. As leaders, we are playing a dangerous game when we don't consider the whole picture.

We are constantly playing "Three Truths and a Lie".

We are always scanning our environments to determine (both for ourselves and for our people) the following:

- Who were we (What made us who we are)?

- Who are we (The person in the mirror today)?

- What do we strive to become (The person we hope to see in the mirror)?

While all incredibly important questions, we are often forced to assume so much about those we lead in order to inspire great results. And while assumption often is given a bad reputation, it is at times needed in order to keep up with our obligations. There have been times that I have made assumptions, often because a quick decision was required and the information was limited. Whenever possible, I strive to find as much detail as I can, especially when the stakes are high. I recommend that you do the same.

Leadership isn't just giving... Leadership isn't just taking... Leadership isn't just speaking... Leadership isn't just listening...

Meaningful leadership is all of the above; and while the philosophy of servant leadership is one that I believe in (I work for the people), I also recognize that I must be working with a purpose based on the questions above. Because people will see through anything false about my actions today. And because people look for alignment in what we all seek to become.

To lead, we must self-actualize constantly, for we cannot successfully lead others without clear understanding of our direction... and ourselves.

To be a leader, you must recognize that you don't know everything. You have to be aware that there is no way you can know everything about your employees, friends, loved ones, and even yourself. Striving for a state of constant discovery will keep you grounded. More importantly, a commitment to constant discovery forces you to listen – and learn.

We all live our lives surrounded by Three Truths and a Lie. Or maybe more than just one... but can you always identify the lie?

LEADERSHIP:
A LEGACY OF INDECISION

Tweet This:

Sometimes the decisions you don't make are more critical than the ones you do.

"Control your own destiny or someone else will."
– Jack Welch #quote

It is a common belief to think that the actions we take and decisions that we make as leaders will be what best defines us throughout our careers.

True perhaps, but actions and decisions are certainly not the entire story.

What if I suggested that the actions we *don't* take and the decisions we *don't* make may very well leave a more lasting legacy than any of the things we actually do?

Consider this:

I have found that as emotional beings, no matter how courageous and fearless we may appear, we have a tendency to show the wrong emotion at the wrong time.

Sympathy rather than empathy, pride rather than acceptance, hubris over humility, and so on and so forth.

These feelings can often lead to indecision, even in many cases where we know what the right decision is. Sometimes, even the best leader is overcome with a certain type of stubbornness that creates less than stellar results.

Let's take our employees for instance. In every organization, the most important component for great success is great people. The subjective philosophy of "people first" comes from the maxim that great ideas come to life with great people. However, even mediocre ideas can thrive with the right team in place. I call this "The People Effect," which basically implies that success is more dependent on great people than great ideas.

But again, with subjectivity often comes "Right Fit." It is entirely possible for an organization to have good talent that doesn't fit. And a misfit can be as problematic as a complete lack of talent.

It isn't uncommon that we onboard personnel who showed a track record of success at a past position, only to be a misfit within our own organization. This situation serves as a great example of a crossroads where indecision can lead us astray.

In leadership, it is our responsibility to bring out the very best in those around us. That outcome happens through setting a great example. And by creating an environment that inspires those within.

However, sometimes we do all that we can and the "Right Fit" just isn't there. Sometimes we must make the hard choice to separate from a hiring decision, because the cost of continuing down that path is too great.

Perhaps that cost appears financially, perhaps intangibly, or maybe even both.

Let's explore this further.

In my career I have been involved with numerous roles where the key limiting factors came down to the decisions that were *not* made.

Take these stories, for example, straight from the archives of my career.

- Early in my career, a thriving company saw turnover at its VP of Sales position. After taking nearly a year to fill the position, a misfit was hired. It took only a month for the global sales organization to realize this fact. However, the company (and its leadership) took more than 2 years to make a change. What was once the industry leader quickly crumbled into a position of near irrelevance as a result. The time where necessary change wasn't made cost the company revenues, customers, and market share.

- I led sales for an emerging start-up with an exciting product and a positive future. The founder of the company was a highly intelligent individual, but not a strong leader. With a short investment runway, the founder gripped tightly to the helm – rather than bringing on an experienced CEO to lead the capitalization of the company. Eventually the cash ran dry, and the founder lost everything – including his title. What he "didn't do" had for more impact than what he did.

- I led an organization with a handful of highly talented sales personnel and a great history of long term customer relationships. These sales leaders provided the company with some impressive revenues. However, the ownership of the company tended to resent the highly paid sales team – rather than embracing their contributions. Further, the company tended to stand loyal to non-producers for a plethora of reasons. After endless diatribes about the risks of not embracing your talent, the company watched its top contributors one after another exit for other opportunities. To this day, the company has struggled in its indecision to let go of weak links. Cultivating the best talent is a key leadership initiative, and their results in this area have been mixed. The ability to let go of under-producers could eventually become the company's demise…

In every one of these cases, the controlling/leading entities were very aware of the problems – yet they chose not to do anything about it. In each case it was bureaucracy, pride, sympathy, or just ignorance that caused this inaction. Nevertheless, these stories become legacies created in indecision.

As a leader, don't allow success or failure to be built in what you didn't do.

When you know the course of action, you must respond promptly to be sure that you are always serving the greater good of the organization.

Perhaps Seth Godin said it best…"You don't need more time, you just need to decide."

LEADERS:
GET BACK TO PUTTING FIRST THINGS FIRST

Tweet This:

Time is one of the few truly fixed resources. You can't make more of it, but you can focus on how you use it.

With the evolution of technology we have become incredibly more productive.

You can read your email while pouring coffee; you can respond on the walk to lunch. Our mobile devices allow us to stay connected to every single thing that is happening every minute of the day. Isn't it great?

It sure is, but would I be stepping out of line if I suggested that all of this productivity is making us wildly unproductive at times? Allow me to explain.

Over the past few years as more and more information has been made available and as the on demand world has led to on demand people we have become increasingly unable to spend adequate time focused on the right things.

However, we have become so unbelievably busy that we feel like we are working non-stop around the clock.

Ultimately, time management is always an issue. However, if we want to see greater levels of success in our businesses we have to go back to one of the simple business rules of business:

"Put First Things First"

The problem is, many of us aren't doing this anymore. Instead, we are putting "First Things in Front of Us First." The key difference here is that the email, tweet, phone call, or person in front of us at any given moment may serve as a good opportunity to feel busy, but this doesn't mean that the activity is the best use of time and resources.

Falling into this trap is easy to do, but there is a way out.

I recently encountered a situation that served as both a good example and inspiration for this chapter. I was speaking with a friend who shared two significant problems he was having with his business. While I won't get specific, the issues were related to a lingering personnel issue, and a forecast/budget planning issue.

Apparently, a member of his leadership team was in charge of completing these key tasks. However these important strategic issues were not being attended to because of continued high levels of "here and now" distractions. Now, several months later, the lingering effect of distraction started to rear its ugly head.

While the flurry of activity may feel like a high level of achievement, let me assure you that activity serves as nothing more than an excuse. "Activity" in itself is not substantial reason for not completing the important strategic tasks at hand. In fact, that approach is leads only to poor long-term business performance. What was even crazier about my friend's situation: the two significant problems could be taken care of with probably one or two focused days of work!

So now we have a frustrated business owner – and an executive that isn't really aware that the job isn't getting done. Frustration reigns because much of the business' daily activity is being driven by external forces.

Bottom line, both my friend and the executive in charge of the strategic activity share some of the blame here. However, blame aside, the "activity" problem is more common than one may think.

The executive is an overall high performer that has been bogged down by "First Thing in Front of Me" overload, and my friend really wants to allow his leadership to move forward without micromanagement.

The Solution: From the top of the organization, you must remind your teams that being busy and being productive are not the same thing. With the unbelievable amount of information available to all of us – along with the mobile tools for accessing that information – we can become captive to the devices that were designed to make us more efficient.

You must remember that businesses have priorities. As a leader, you are accountable for keeping "First Things First." While there is no de facto way to handle the information overload, I have spoken to many executives who only respond to email twice a day, or only return calls during a designated period (barring an emergency, of course). I have had to do this myself, to avoid being overrun by the flow of incoming communications.

When determining how to get your time back under control, remember: the overarching idea is to not allow other peoples' priorities to constantly supersede your own. Don't get distracted from what must come first.

So the next time your email dings, your text bings, your phone rings, or your tweet sings, do you have the discipline to stay on task?

SERVANT LEADERSHIP:
FLIP THE ORG CHART

Tweet This:

Ultimately we all serve the client. Therefore leaders must serve those who serve the customers.

Servant leadership is incredibly rewarding because it builds a level or trust and reciprocity that can never be created through a traditional organizational hierarchy.

The tenants of servant leadership are really quite simple. The premise is built on an upside-down organizational model. The top of the org chart is represented by the customer, front line workers and managers. The executives and senior managers live at the very bottom of the organization. This is because in the servant leadership model the executives work for "the people."

As I mentioned before, it is in such an upside-down environment where talented people tend to achieve the greatest results. Success is rooted in the organization providing the team with the correct support in order to create the desired result.

However, for an organization to effectively achieve the benefits of servant leadership, there are tenets that exist and rules that apply. First there are tenets of the organization.

By definition, the organization must subscribe to these ideas. Then, there are rules related to the quality of people in which the company employs.

Without the right mix of these two fundamentals, the benefits of servant leadership will rarely (if ever) be fully realized.

First, the organizational tenets:

- **Consistency** – Servant leadership cannot only exist amongst the most senior leaders. Servant leadership must exist at every level, to enable the employees throughout the entire organization. Without consistency, leadership becomes more and more stringent, as processes move throughout an organization. This managerial design and execution leads to highly-empowered senior leaders and a micro-managed and resentful front line.

- **Empowerment** – More than just the act of delegation, the servant leader must genuinely empower, endure failure, and even take blame for the shortcomings of the team. I have long believed that real relationships and trust are most often built in the proverbial foxhole. When your team sees your commitment during the tough times, it builds an unwavering loyalty.

- **Commitment** – A team that subscribes to the upside-down organization has to be heavily committed to this philosophy. The company must be committed to the recruiting, training, retaining, and – more than anything – defining a culture where the employee is the leader. This culture is built on consistency and commitment. Building an organization of employees who believe in their leadership starts with the company's vision (that's the role of the leader!) and is reflected in every activity that the company performs.

A consistently empowering organization that commits itself to serving its people has the foundation of great results. However, the organization must also have the right people on board in order to create those results.

I refer to this empowerment equation as the DNA of a great hire. And these great hires are the types of employees required to reap the benefits of servant leadership. Below are three key traits found in this type of employee:

- **Motivated** – To benefit from enablement, and an empowered environment, the employee must be motivated. While motivation alone will not guarantee success, it is required as part of its foundation. Servant leaders will rarely provide you with a list of instructions, but rather a nudge in the right direction. Whether or not you arrive will be entirely up to you.

- **Dedicated** – Not just dedicated to the job, but a new hire must be dedicated to the company and its vision. Enlightenment comes from failures (note empowerment above) as much as anything and some employees will become disenchanted when they aren't immediately successful. But to truly learn, the student must want to learn (motivated) and be willing to put in the work (dedicated). True for employees as well.

- **Competent** – The "Peter Principle" talks about the employee being promoted up to their own level of incompetency. Well, an incompetent employee will likely struggle even more immensely with great servant leadership. It does take "enough" of the right ability to overcome this tendency. With the right basic knowledge, combined with the traits above, the employee is in a perfect place to benefit from servant leadership.

Like most business practices, the three organizational tenets and the three DNA traits will never guarantee success. However, I firmly believe that they serve as the foundation within a servant leadership organization.

Like a strategy without execution, a great servant leader will likely fail if those he leads are not dedicated to the cause. What is your organization's cause?

It is your job to earn the commitment from your people, as a leader, to back these causes. That "cause" is the reason your company exists! Servant leaders shine a light on the cause, and make believers out of everyone that they work FOR.

THREE WAYS
TO REPLACE "BUSY"
WITH "EFFECTIVE"

Tweet This:

I don't care if you work 40 hours, I care that you are meeting expectations. It is that simple.

If I had to assess the first place that most managers go wrong, I could come up with a few ideas. Perhaps it is the misunderstanding of power, or maybe the desire to micromanage every little activity. While both of these impulses certainly rear their ugly head via our leaders and managers, I'd like to propose an alternative to your first mistake.

From the time that we were small children, we were told by our parents, teachers, and coaches the following..." We just want to see you give it your best," or "Work hard and the results will follow." Sadly, this sage advice turns out to be as wrong as fried bacon.

Hard work is an important ingredient to success, that's no secret. However, I'm just saying that hard work is often misinterpreted *as* success. Effort is sometimes masked in a state of busy-ness that isn't even hard work at all – let alone effective.

Instead, I'd like to transform the lifelong advice given above to the new society without red pens. Consider the following perspective, with a Millennial twist:

- Is an F in school okay so long as the student tried their best?

- Do we not have to pay our bills so long as we made our best effort?

- Does trying hard generate positive cash flow so we can run our businesses?

While every exception has its rule, the overwhelming answer to these questions is no.

If you attempted to justify them with a "yes" your results would be a high school drop out that can't pay his bills because his lemonade stand got shut down.

Oversimplified? Perhaps, but nevertheless the point remains the same.

When it comes to leading people I have been adamant from the beginning that I really don't care how long you work, as long as you meet your objectives. While every situation is unique, in general terms I mean the following:

- If you are in sales: meet your quota

- If you are in an administrative function: finish your tasks

- If you are in management: value your time and the time of others

I've gone so far as to tell a few "rainmaking" sales folks that if they hit their sales quota in August they can golf until December. While I say this somewhat in jest (some of these folks don't play golf), the point isn't lost on them.

When I mention this to some managers, they say that if the employee quickly hits their targets then the manager should push for more productivity. I agree, in part, but I with a caveat. If your employee knows that finishing in a timely manner is simply going to yield additional demand on them, you may not get them very excited about overachieving. In order to maximize both time and results, leaders must make sure the effort is worthwhile to the employee. If an employee is easily hitting their targets, then perhaps (over time) they need escalated goals to make sure they are challenged. Of course this increase should coincide with their professional and financial growth.

The demand that managers tend to put on their people can create a flurry of activity, yet little additional productivity. In the end, being really busy in itself doesn't pay bills, doesn't foster innovation, and doesn't strengthen culture. In fact, too much busy-ness may in fact weaken the culture and productivity.

Try replacing "busy" with the following three things to yield greater results:

1. **Trade Clocks for Outcomes:** Time is finite. In fact, none of us can make more time – and that's what makes

it precious. Talk to most employees about their vacation, and they will tell you how important "their" time is. Well, many employees would be inspired by the opportunity to create a little flex time. So, perhaps instead of punching a clock, start focusing on what needs to be done each day, week and month, before someone has reached their targets. Once those targets are achieved, allow the employee to earn some personal time in exchange for their efficiency. Everyone wins; the company is executing its objectives and the employee is getting something precious in return.

2. **Reward Efficiency:** Beyond time, efficiency can be rewarded in many ways. When targets, objectives and revenues are realized, companies know they are making money. While sharing the wealth may be outlandish, most business owners would share a piece of a bigger pie all day long. Highly efficient employees tend to drive dollars to the bottom line; make sure they see that their contribution matters. Telling employees that they matter will get you some bonus points; showing them they matter will get you some bonus hours.

3. **Live the Message:** This leadership insight is a life lesson; it applies here and in so many other places. So ask yourself often, "What does your team see when they see you?" If they don't see you living the message, then you can bet they won't be as likely to either. As a leader, you need to be on time (as much as possible), show respect and value for others' time (regardless of whether they are subordinates or not). Consistently discuss the importance of goals, what they are, and where you and your team are in respect to meeting them.

As long as you play within the laws and the moral fibers that guide you, results trump activity every time. So starting today, get busy on being effective.

SO YOU THINK YOU WANT TO LEAD?

Tweet This:

Leadership is so often mistaken for power and fame. For most leaders that recognition doesn't come until much later-if at all.

Everybody wants to be a leader, or so they say. There is a misnomer when it comes to what leadership is that people think that being in a position of power makes you a leader. While position can give you power, it does not create real influence. Only through your words (and much more importantly, your actions) can you truly become a leader. So you think you want to lead? First ask yourself these four questions.

1. As a leader, do my followers work for me, or do I work for them?

2. As a leader, do I seek to enrich the lives of others or myself first?

3. As a leader, do I aspire to be liked or respected?

4. As a leader, am I willing to give credit to others for success, and accept the blame for when we fail?

What are your answers? Here are mine…

1. *As a leader I work for my followers.* To guide, to inspire, to motivate. It isn't about me, it is about them.

2. *As a leader, I become enriched through enriching the lives of others.* If my priorities are first, then what I am doing is not leadership.

3. *As a leader I know I cannot be liked by all.* Seeking to be liked should not be the goal. It may happen from time to time; however, I seek to be respected as an honest, fair, and empathetic leader that motivates and drives the highest level of performance from my team.

4. *As a leader I am willing to fall on my sword.* I am willing to defer credit, and take blame to yield greater outcomes.

So You Think You Want to Lead? Why?

It seems all too often that people land themselves in a position and become entirely complacent with the situation. Whether sales, marketing, support, management, or other, it is important to never accept things as they are. You must always continue to aspire to be better at what you do.

In today's competitive marketplace companies seek employees that not only work hard, but those who have the initiative and drive to learn everything about the job that they do. Furthermore, companies aspire to find employees who are creative and imaginative; simply being competent is no longer good enough.

This begs the question... Do you want to be indispensable to your organization? Here are four questions that you need to be able to answer with **YES** if you want to go from currently employed to forever employable.

- Are you always looking for ways to be better at what you do?

- Do you take initiative to solve problems?

- Do you embrace learning opportunities?

- Are you willing to embrace change?

Can you say yes to all of the above? Whether yes or no, I suggest each and every day that you aspire to learn something new to hone your craft and be the best at whatever it is that you do.

Simply put, being a taskmaster no longer cuts it. The game changer is attitude. There are plenty of people who can "do the job," but companies want more than that.

If you are serious about success then be prepared to answer this: What do you bring to the table that makes you indispensable?

FINANCIAL LEADERSHIP:
SIX REASONS TO HIRE A GREAT CFO

Tweet This:

Great leaders surround themselves with great leaders. Who surrounds you?

In the lifecycle of a growing business, there may be nothing more commonly overlooked than financial leadership.

In today's fast-paced world of the overnight entrepreneur, sales is the game, and marketing is the vehicle. But unless your business is all pre-pay, cash flow can be a huge limiting factor in successfully managing the growth of your organization. During periods of rapid growth, especially in a business that is capital intensive, all the sales in the world will not take your business to the next level. If you aren't careful, growth can actually put you out of business.

In today's market, proper capitalization is becoming more and more rare. The current economic circumstances have brought a new need to the surface: the requirement for strong, creative financial leaders that can do more with less.

For this reason, there may be no position more critical (and perhaps more misunderstood in the growing organization) than the CFO.

Let's take a look at some of the more prevalent CFO misconceptions:

- The CFO is nothing more than a glorified accountant/ bookkeeper.

- The CFO is only there to thwart expenses and keep a company thrifty on expenditures.

- The CFO does the work that the CEO doesn't care to.

In some businesses, the "CFO" may certainly have some mundane tasks; actually, that's a universal truth for any position. However, the CFO in any forward thinking organization is far from just a bookkeeper.

It's the responsibility of every employee to spend wisely. Many times the CFO is there to do much of what the CEO cannot do. (Sometimes due to lack of time or lack of know how.)

As the world's CEOs and CMOs are taking the market by storm and driving customers to the door, behind each of them (the successful ones at least) you will find a CFO that makes it all possible. Nevertheless, the average employee often has no idea what the CFO does, making the position not only underappreciated, but undervalued.

Now that these myths have been debunked, let's discuss the core of financial leadership – and answer an important question.

Why must an organization, especially a growing one, have a great CFO?

- **Capability:** The ideal CFO can tell you (based upon your current capital structure) exactly what the organization can do, financially. Capability is key to moving an organization forward, so it doesn't get out over its skis...

- **Planning:** The ideal CFO can analyze the current mix of business and provide the sales and strategist with the foresight required to properly plan for growth. A plan that cannot be funded is also referred to as a pipe dream.

- **Alignment:** In the case of companies that have substantial growth and capital requirement the ideal CFO can align the company's cash resources to the plan.

- **Communication:** Both internal to other leadership as well as external to banks, investors, and partners, the ideal CFO can instill confidence with key stakeholders (both internal and external) to drive things forward.

- **Execution:** A strategy is ultimately only as good as its execution. Without the right financial leadership, you can sell yourself out of business. To execute the business plan, finance must be in lock step with everyone else.

- **Focus:** Unless you are in the business of financial services, finance is not in itself the business. As a leader, you want to be able to focus on what it is you do – and know the money is handled. That support is priceless!

When a company has strong financial leadership, it is rarely noticed or appreciated by the working majority. However, when that ideal CFO leadership is missing it exposes everyone from top to bottom. For an organization to achieve its goals, it requires careful planning and extraordinary execution. Neither is even remotely possible without a highly capable CFO.

By most standards, finance may never be seen as the sexy part of the business. But if you try to grow a business without great financial leadership, you will quickly realize that financial strength may be the most important part.

THE LEADERSHIP TRUST TEST: 10 QUESTIONS

Tweet This:

Are you trusted by those you serve? You better be. But how do you know?

If you had to identify a single thing that the great leaders of commerce, war, sports, and politics all had in common, what would you say?

Would you reference charisma, or strategy? Perhaps persistence or dedication?

To all of the aforementioned traits I would respond with a definite maybe.

Nonetheless, I would say that leaders all share some of these characteristics. But the great ones had something else. This "something else" is the key component to great relationships – relationships which have forever served as the foundation of success for leaders.

Trust, and nothing else, is far and away the most critical component of successful leadership. If you doubt this even for a moment, then think about the last time you accomplished something great where trust was lacking among the stakeholders? I tried to think of such an instance, and was left without a single example.

At the very foundation of every relationship lies this deeply felt (yet superficially undetectable) guiding element. The feeling of trust (or lack thereof) defines your relationships, and your results.

The great leaders have trust, but do you? Do you inspire trust?

Here are 10 questions you can ask to determine how trusted you are. If you can honestly answer yes to all 10, then you are on your way to becoming one of the great ones.

- Would your employees agree with the statement, "You are transparent with your communication"?

- Do your customers consider the deal done when you shake hands or when the contract is signed?

- Are you able to influence and maintain strong morale during times of adversity?

- Can you be direct in your communication or do you often have to walk on eggshells not to offend?

- When you introduce change, does your team show (through their actions) a willingness to go along?

- Will your team members challenge your ideas freely?

- Do those you lead understand your plan and know your means of measurement?

- When goals and objectives aren't met, do you point the first finger at yourself?

- Would your team agree with the following statement: "You have never lied to them"?

- Most Importantly: Would YOU trust YOU? (Be honest now)

These questions alone aren't the only indication of whether or not you can be, should be, or are trusted. However, a bit of introspection and consideration of those you lead are a tremendous way to measure the level of trust you have.

What I know for sure is that trust is the single most important piece in solving the leadership puzzle. If you have trust, you can effortlessly impact change and influence people. Without it, you will find even the smallest shift can cause a backbreaking ripple in your organization.

Are you the trusted piece of the puzzle that makes it whole? It all begins with trust.

SIX THINGS THAT STRONG LEADERS DO DIFFERENTLY

Tweet This:

There are many traits and behaviors that can be attributed to most leaders. But what do the best leaders do differently?

While I believe that leadership can be learned, I have found that the practice of leadership is rarely successful via the application of textbook principles. As someone who has studied, taught, and practiced leadership, I can tell you that there are thousands of leadership principles. Most of these principles can be found in a million books and seminars on leadership, and its surrounding ideology.

However, in-depth training and knowledge of leadership practices isn't what true leadership is all about.

Leadership occurs in the inherent actions and subconscious beliefs of the leader. These actions and beliefs make all the difference in the world. While there are countless things that individual leaders do drive performance and behavior, there are also some things that are more consistent among strong leaders. Here are six things that strong leaders do differently:

58

- **Embrace Adversity:** When the world is good, anyone can lead. You rarely see ball players and coaches having a sideline fight during a victory. Winning behavior translates straight from the field to the office as well. Leaders that know how to not only weather the storm, but keep a watchful eye on the horizon, tend to drive the most successful outcomes.

- **Transparency:** Too often I find managers and leaders that limit the communication they provide to their team. Sometimes limitations occur for monetary reasons – such as limiting awareness to profits or perhaps losses. Other times, limited communication is to keep employees strategically unaware of the plan or direction that the company is taking (such as a pending merger or acquisition). Whatever the reason, I have rarely found that limiting information is a good plan. In fact, I believe employees (people) are incredibly intelligent and they almost always see through the lack of transparency. What is worse than communication? The lack of it leaves your team to make their own assertions – assertions that can be devastating to productivity and morale. Strong leaders know how to be transparent without putting the organization at risk.

- **Empathetic Ear:** Have you ever left a conversation or a meeting where you feel like you were talked to death? Either talked to or talked at, but nonetheless you feel as if you were asked to drink from a fire hose, perhaps without even being thirsty. Strong leaders understand that talking is not the means to gathering support, or the desired results, from the team. I'm not trying to say that a strong leader doesn't have important things to share.

But you – as a strong leader – have to know that what you want to share will be much better received when your team feels understood. This tenet of understanding and empathy transcends every silo of our life – from work to family to community. Those leaders we support generally serve our interests more than their own.

- **Surrounded With Brilliance:** The inherent leader knows one thing for sure… that they don't know everything. Michael Jordan, arguably the best basketball player to ever play the game, didn't win a championship before Scotty Pippen arrived. In business, great leaders may get the credit – but rarely because they knew how to do it all - and did it all – themselves. Rather, success is a result of the fact that the business leader knew some of it and left the rest to the experts. The best leaders know what holes they need to fill. Strong leaders spend a tremendous amount of time and energy to make sure that they those holes with brilliance and expertise. Show me a great leader in sports, military, politics, or business and I'll name at least one person in their immediate circle that was of great significance to their success.

- **Many Shades of Gray:** Most managers live for black and white. They seek out simple answers and avoid areas that cannot be easily defined. A better manager realizes that success isn't so simple. However, team leaders can often get stuck in the gray area that lives between black and white. The best leaders recognize that there are far more than 50 shades of gray. These shades of gray provoke the leader to ask more questions, listen more empathetically, and guide their team to the next destination.

- **Adaptable:** For the longest time I was certain that better leaders understood the importance of staying the course. (A "Seven Habits-esque" fashion of write the plan and live the plan). As I've experienced life, I have found that this "write the plan, live the plan" theory, while sound in many ways, is missing a key component. This key component is what drives better leadership. The missing ingredient? The strong leader has a plan and commits to the plan, but knows when the plan needs altering. The strong leader is quick to make adjustments. There are two major points in which most plans and strategies go wrong. One is the early diversion that is created by lack of immediate results. The second is the late turn, which often involves trying to redirect the Titanic after it has already hit the iceberg. For best results, leaders must know when to stay the course because the strategy is working - and when to steer away from the proverbial iceberg before it's too late.

Leaders come in all shapes and sizes, from all walks of life. While some are better than others, all leaders have certain characteristics that drive them to be more successful.

These great leadership traits have risks. And while I expect to see all of these traits from anyone whom I follow, it begs the question, is there any downside to leading with character?

RISKS OF HUMILITY

- If I am humble... will this be mistaken for a lack of confidence?
- If I am humble... will people not believe I have accomplished much?
- If I am humble... will I not stand out?

RISKS OF HONESTY

- If I am honest... will I miss a shortcut?
- If I am honest... will others want to hear the truth?
- If I am honest... may others lie and get ahead?

RISKS OF EMPATHY

- If I show empathy... will others try to walk all over me?
- If I show empathy... will it be mistaken for sympathy?
- If I show empathy... will I be perceived as indecisive?

RISKS OF INTEGRITY

- If I have high integrity... will the "less" moral pass me by?
- If I have high integrity... will doing the right thing cost me in the short run?
- If I have high integrity... will it go unnoticed in an often amoral society?

What are your answers?

VALUE *NOT* ADDED

Tweet This:

Doing exactly what is expected of you isn't a value add. No matter how hard you try to convince yourself that it is.

It seems as if every couple of years the brethren of Harvard Business Review come up with a buzzword to preoccupy industry.

Almost in "Wag the Dog" fashion, the words take hold and prevent us from thinking clearly about what it is we really do that would make a customer want to work with us.

Instead, sentences littered with buzzwords plaster themselves across our company mission statements, websites, and marketing collateral. Hiding behind these buzzwords, we try to distract our customers from the fact that we have (in many cases) become increasingly the same, rather than distinctive, in what we do.

From small business to Fortune 1000 enterprises, we have not been shy about adopting the buzzwords into our business plans. As interchangeable as bottled water, the term "value add," is a phrase we all use. We march into scope reviews, customer briefings, and design build proposals preaching the value we create through a high-touch, customer-oriented approach that yields great results for clients.

The problem is, what is being proclaimed as "value add" in many cases is becoming more and more what is simply expected from us. Last I checked, value add isn't founded in doing what is expected, yet rather in (wait for it) adding value *above and beyond*. Simple? Yes, but sadly added value is not often accomplished.

While there is really nothing wrong with stating your business philosophy, the aforementioned focus on high touch, customer-oriented approach is only a problem that we are mistaking as true value added.

Where does this incongruent use of terminology come from, and how do we stop it in order to pave the way for real value creation?

First, we need to take into consideration what is the "norm" in our respective industries. If your organization is trying to sell the concept of what is typical and expected from a business of your type (e.g. customer service or trained technical resources) you need to reconsider. While that concept may indeed be part of your core business philosophy, it is not truly an added value.

Second, we need to think about what we actually do that is different. Dig a little bit deeper into your bag of tricks and discuss one or two things that truly allow your organization to be different than your competitors. For instance, great customer service is not in itself a value added. However, if you can say you respond to 100 percent of customer service inquiries within 30 minutes while the industry average is 8 hours, you would truly be different – and that adds value.

Third and perhaps most importantly, ask your clients what it is that makes you better. We spend so much time subscribing to what we think makes us better that we forget we aren't the ones who truly decide. Most of your customers have tried other suppliers and have had varying experiences with them. Beyond just the old testimonial, ask them what it is that makes your organization different.

What is the value that your clients see in continuing to work with you? You will be amazed at what you can learn from asking those who are already your customers. What is even more amazing is how often we forget to ask.

Don't miss this opportunity, a wealth of knowledge awaits.

The fact is, the more we dig our heels into the ground and proclaim our value added, the less it seems we pay attention to what the real value is.

There is a reason your business has grown, thrived, or at very least survived. However, the reason may not be what you think it is. In fairness to you, your employees, and your customers, it is time to reevaluate your value – that value makes you different, better, and truly important to your customer.

While words like synergy, core competency and yes, "value added", may have riddled our communities, remember there is real value in what you do.

Harvard doesn't have the answer for you; it's your customers and employees. Ultimately, ask your customer for their ideas. Your biggest successes and failures will yield the best understanding.

FIVE HABITS OF GREAT EXECUTION

Tweet This:

Ultimately your leadership will be graded on how well your teams execute.

In the new world we move fast. We seek to rapidly meet objectives and achieve success with every idea, as soon as the idea is generated.

If strategy is the engine that drives business success, then execution is the oil that keeps the engine lubricated. And without oil, even the most perfectly tuned Ferrari becomes merely a beautiful chair – a facade of a once mighty rocket on four wheels.

Like the metaphorical Ferrari, a business cannot operate on strategy alone. Execution is the key, and execution is the most often ignored piece to what is really a simple formula for business success.

I propose the simple math... (Assuming the company has proper resources for strategy implementation)

Strategy + Execution = Results

Simple enough right? However there are a handful of variables that can yield various results such as...

Good Strategy + Poor Execution =
Lower Than Expected Results

Even as far as to say...

Perfect Strategy (if there was such a thing) +
Poor Execution =
Lower than Expected Results

Is it out of sorts to say that the perfect strategy without the proper expectation will not yield the expected result? I would feel entirely confident in the statement. In fact if you asked just about any CEO or other executive I would suggest they would agree without a second thought.

So let's look at the other side: can a poor strategy with great execution yield better than expected results?

I would be remiss to say that anyone knowingly goes to market with a bad strategy. However, all strategies are not created equally. Sometimes limited resources or a contracting market can hinder a situation, leaving management with few options. Resource challenges create a difficult road to achieving the required results.

At this point, execution becomes the critical next step in a company life cycle. In fact I am confident in saying that a mediocre strategy can be executed so well that it drives extraordinary results. However, in order to achieve great results we must execute.

To execute well, we MUST do the following five things:

1. **Communicate:** I can't even begin to tell you how many times I have spoken to an employee who could not even begin to articulate the strategic vision of their company. While not every employee may have direct input into the strategy itself, it is the sum of the employees' contribution in conjunction with the strategy that ultimately yields an outcome. So many ideas, visions, and strategies are built in the boardroom and never make it to the work force. Vision is never delivered via osmosis, and execution is never accomplished in a vacuum.

2. **"Buy In":** I put quotations around this one and here's why: The leadership professor may say you need complete buy in for organizational success. To that I say, "UNLIKELY!"

   However, to maximize strategic outcomes you need your most influential team members to contribute at a high level. While it is ideal to have everyone believe, if you have more than a handful of employees, getting collective buy in up front is quite unrealistic. That consensus is why there must be a targeted group within any organization. I'll call this targeted group "the influential". This group is comprised of the most critical personnel in the execution process. These thought-leaders need to be identified during the strategy design phase. Ideally, their input to secure true buy in is crucial as the strategy is rolled out. Successful execution is dependent upon the influential buy in.

3. **Benchmarks:** While the plan may have some expected end result, rarely is a strategy implemented in a window

so small that benchmarks don't need to be set. Many strategies are filled with revenue and profit benchmarks which serve as a good start. However, I recommend tangible targets that augment revenue and profit, in order to see that the plan is on track. These targets can include production levels, customer satisfaction levels, brand awareness, or other metrics. Profit and revenue are the ultimate goals, but sometimes you have to build the roads before you can drive on them.

4. **Flexibility:** Some of the best plans crumble under the pressure of execution. If the strategists are the "coaches" then the employees are the players on the field. When the quarterback snaps the ball and the defense is already in the backfield, it takes a rapid adjustment to save the play from being a disaster. To execute you need to be able to change course to keep the plan on track. Sometimes you need to tuck the ball and prevent a turnover. Nonetheless, if you force the strategy without being flexible, you may end up taking multiple steps backwards – and sabotaging whatever progress has been made.

5. **Discipline:** I call discipline a lost art. We have become "Shiny Object Chasers," and we find ourselves changing course with every change in the jet stream. The companies that I have seen execute more successfully than all the rest are the ones that see the goal, and stay the course. However, having discipline doesn't mean that you can't be flexible. But discipline means being deliberate in your approach. And discipline helps you to realize that programs and products take time. Part of navigating a course involves minor corrections along the

way, and not losing sight of the end goal. I've seen many companies expect results in an unrealistic timeframe, and that's not discipline. True leaders tend to be acutely aware of their objectives and they are almost painstakingly focused on accomplishing them. When changing course, they can be flexible but stay entirely disciplined on their objectives.

Companies like Cisco, Apple, Berkshire, and others all have uncanny discipline to stay and execute along the strategic course.

THREE COMPETITORS
WE ALL FACE

Tweet This:

The phenomenon of comparing ourselves to the wrong competitors is a risk. Start with you and what you can control!

Walk up to your average entrepreneur, sales executive, or marketer and ask them who their biggest competitor is.

I'd be willing to bet (with odds in your favor) that 9 out of 10 of them will name another company. Likely a company in the exact same line of business as yours, serving the exact same geographic customer.

I'd also be willing to bet you, with those same odds, that the person is right about one thing and wrong about another. The named business does represent competition. But by no means are they naming their "biggest" competitor.

In every role I've worked in I have had numerous sales personnel and other leadership team members constantly focusing on the obvious competitors. In some cases, the focus became somewhat unhealthy and potentially paralyzing. So much energy was spent on these proposed rivals that it became our entire business purpose to unseat them.

I guess the thought was, "if we beat them we were guaranteed success." However, that mindset puts a lot of eggs into another company's strategy!

Maybe we need to first forget the competition. Sound like a radical idea? Well, before we can worry about the others in our industry we must focus on ourselves and our business execution. I stick to that sentiment in respect to worrying about other companies.

While some competition needs to be faced all the time, it just may not be the competition that you imagine.

In actuality, we all face three competitors in business. No matter what your business or industry, those three competitors are exactly the same.

- **Don't Know:** Whether it is the market you serve, your value proposition, or the customer sentiment about your product, "don't know" is one of your greatest competitors. The most common "don't know" question is: Do your best potential customers even know you exist? Your landscape is full of the unknown, and those gaps must be filled. The inability to recognize how "don't know" is effecting your business is quietly costing you sales (and profits) every day.

- **Do Nothing:** Sometimes you do know your biggest challenges, shortcomings, or opportunities. But what if you choose to do nothing about them? Often "do nothing" is a subconscious choice. Sometimes, inaction is a matter of being stubborn, uncertain, or afraid. Nevertheless, if you "do nothing" it is unlikely you will move to or stay in the front of the pack. Just ask Polaroid after they created the technology to do digital images, but chose to do nothing and protect their legacy film business.

- **Don't Care:** Most often, indifference isn't an internal problem but an external one. Perhaps you think you know your customer – but your offering isn't what the people want. You could have the most brilliant geniuses in the world working on amazingly complex solutions, but if you are solving the wrong problem... Well, you will have a lot of brilliantly bad offerings. The result is customers that will never support your brand, or even worse... indifference. That's the danger of "don't care" – you're on the path to being forgotten.)

To that indifference I say: the opportunist is the one that sees where the real competition lies. For now, the three most important competitors above can be our little secret. We will let everyone else believe that competition is just another business – but we know better!

YOUR PERCEPTION *IS* YOUR REALITY

Tweet This:

Right, wrong, or indifferent. You choose how you view the world.

A huge portion of our lives is comprised of a vast number of interactions. In some cases, these interactions are small conversations. In other cases, these interactions are substantial dialogues. Regardless, in every interaction there is someone delivering the message (the person speaking or writing) and someone receiving it (the reader, the listener, the audience).

With this in mind, have you ever thought about how many ways a single message can be interpreted?

Perception is reality... right?

A mentor once told me that the same message can create hundreds of unique actions. These actions are based on unique perspectives. Putting it into a selling point of view he would say, "You can tell a person to go to hell in one way, and get punched in the nose. Yet you can say virtually the same thing in another way, and the person will ask you to escort them and their bags."

Stay with me here…

In marketing communications, a key concept is the encoding/decoding of messages as it relates to the target audience. The idea here is consistency: a message that is clearly articulated, via the chosen medium, to make sure that the ultimate reaction received is in line with the reaction that the marketer intended to create.

Marketing studies also introduce the concept of "noise" into this equation. Noise is representative of anything that creates ambiguity between the marketer and their message. Essentially, noise is an enemy to the marketer's efforts.

From an oversimplified standpoint the concept is true. The message, much like the game of "Telephone" that we played as children, is best served when the story is heard exactly the same by both the messenger and the receiver.

Remember "Telephone"? In Telephone, a message is put in one person's ear and then passed through several others. Then, the final message at the other end is shared with the group. The final message is often very different than the initial message delivered.

While idealistic, this type of consistent messaging hardly ever happens in business. The main culprit isn't noise, but one key component of communication.

PERCEPTIONS

Perceptions are derived from many things. Attitudes, Values, and Beliefs (among other things) are the building blocks of perception. In many ways, a brand's success or failure isn't always tied to the message created. No, a brand's success is linked to the perception that they create. That maxim holds true for a personal brand as well as a corporate one.

When dealing with people (and brands) that we trust, we tend to take messages at face value. At times we may even glorify the message, because of the source. (Apple, anyone?)

When we hear from a source that's not as trusted or respected, we often see the worst in the message – regardless of its intent or context.

Rush Limbaugh is an example of a polarizing messenger. His fans enjoy his perspective; his detractors dismiss whatever he says. While I'm not trying to offer opinions on talk radio show hosts, Rush represents a wide array of responses on any number of topics.

People who tend to perceive Rush as a crazy conservative have already decided his intent. And chances are his supporters don't see any harm in his comments. The same can be said for our candidates.

Perception plays a part in media, branding and advertising every day. However, perception also hits closer to home.

Recently I received an email from someone that was checking in to see how I was doing – as well as looking for some very specific feedback in regards to something very personal to me. While this person and I have a superficially amicable relationship, I have been troubled by several personal encounters as well as a handful of actions that this person has taken toward others whom I trust.

The email itself was well written and polite; however, my immediate reaction toward the message was inherently negative. The reaction was totally due to the fact that my perception of the person caused me to question their character and their ethics.

For all I know, the person could be genuinely interested in checking in, and could be doing it entirely with good intentions. But my perception told me something different.

As an exercise, think of a person that you trust emphatically... as well as someone whom you generally dislike.

Now say that both of them called you up to see how you were doing or you ran into them. If both were to approach you and deliver to you the exact same message, how would you react? Would it be similar or different? Why?

Regardless of what was said to you, I propose that you would respond much more positively to the trusted person, rather than the disliked person.

Why?

Most simply: your response is based on your perception of the messenger. You perceive the first person as trustworthy, and therefore you trust their input. With the second, your predetermined notions derail the message in its entirety – regardless of intent.

So yes, perception is reality. But moreover: YOUR perception is YOUR reality. With so many messages competing for our attention, our view (and how others view us) is being shaped more rapidly than ever before. These constant perceptions are serving both as an opportunity, and as a risk.

As individuals (and for companies and their brands) we must ask ourselves...

- *What are we doing to earn trust and respect?*

- *How are we shaping our message for our audience?*

- *What are we doing to be sure it is delivered the way we intend?*

- *Are we cognizant of how we are perceived? Are we sure?*

Gary Vaynerchuk was quoted saying "It's never the platform, it's always the message." For me, being more of an "And/Also thinker" I say it's both... so long as the receiver of the message perceives the source the way they want them to.

BUSINESS:
TO SUCCEED, YOU MUST ASK THE RIGHT QUESTIONS

Tweet This:

Replace statements with questions and be amazed at how it changes your approach and more importantly your results.

Our businesses are full of smart people and we are supported by even smarter technology.

Technology has opened a world of possibilities for the organization. Real time, on-demand information tells us everything that is going on with our business.

Real time sales, financials, analytics, and a world of other reports. Where you want it, when you want it.

These tools can all be great for business.

However, the keyword here is *"can"*.

From the time I was a child my father used to always tell me, "The numbers don't lie."

My dad was an entrepreneur. An entrepreneur that pulled himself up by his bootstraps and built a successful business out of sheer grit and determination. With little formal education beyond high school, he became convinced the numbers were the story.

Now that I've gained a bit more experience, I'm pretty certain that much of what he said was correct. The numbers do not lie. In fact, they are the most completely accurate representation of what is going on in a business.

However, the fact that the numbers don't lie doesn't necessarily mean that they are useful. The numbers that are spit out at us via ERP, CRM, EDI, and a vast array of other systems are the words that tell a story. This story requires deciphering. The decoding and interpretation of the numbers comes via a word key that is generated by the organizations' people. Every report, the balance sheet, the income statement, the revenue analysis: all of them tell a story, but how do we determine what that story is?

Here is where better leaders set themselves apart.

Success is not determined by the numbers – we all have the numbers right in front of us. Success is determined by the interpretation of the numbers. Success depends on the questions we ask.

With the right questions we are able to recognize trends, identify plans and strategies, create KPIs, and execute to our plan. The continuous flow of data to our inbox allows us to continue shaping our visions and determine what the next question should be. From those next questions, we continue to arrive at better outcomes.

With the right questions we can control our circumstances.

However, if we ask the wrong questions (or perhaps worse yet, no questions), we become constrained by circumstances. The numbers begin to control us.

Take for example a three-year revenue trend. Let's say that the report shows sales rising by 5%.

For some companies they will look at that and assume that everything is good. Revenue is up, and life is grand.

Consider this viewpoint, and begin asking the right questions:

- **Big Picture Question:** Why is revenue up?

- **Second Level Questions:** Is the increase related to new customers (Width), or more business from current customers (Depth)? Did margin increase or decrease (Profitability)? Was there a significant (perhaps beyond normal) large deal or two that created the higher revenue?

- **Third Level Questions:** What trends can we identify (External, Internal Environment)? What if there are no giant deals next year (Risk Assessment)? What customers fell off (Opportunities)?

The depth of questions could go on and on, but with the "Right Questions" comes better business insight – insight, not numbers, is what propels an organization forward.

With this in mind, let's talk a bit more about the example above...

If the answers to those multi-level questions showed that the business growth was related to one extremely large deal from a current customer, a big-deal repeat is highly unlikely. You may come to realize that your run rate business was actually down year over year, and that you need to generate a plan to offset that big deal that won't return anytime soon. You may have realized that several large customers saw significant drop off in business and that they need some attention because they may have moved a portion of their business to someone else.

And with that movement lies the foundation of the story, and the root of better business execution.

Every day we are bombarded with data that can be used to help us run better organizations and drive more desirable outcomes. However, do not be fooled about the path. The results do not lie within the data you are provided, but rather within the questions that this information drives.

Smart systems and smart people can give you all the tools you need. But only smart leaders know they must ask great questions.

Dad, you were right when you said that the numbers don't lie. However, I hope you realize it was the questions you then asked that made you a success – not just those numbers themselves.

FIVE LEADERSHIP LESSONS YOU CAN ONLY GET FROM EXPERIENCE

Tweet This:

There is no substitute for experience. So don't forget to embrace it!

There's an age-old debate about whether or not leaders can be made, or if you have to be born that way. Nevertheless, every year, countless professionals of all experience levels and all walks of life decide to invest in themselves, to hopefully become the next great leader.

There are a plethora of degrees, certificates, specializations, seminars and other educational means available to learners today. Often times, they are meant to serve as the next check mark in their road to prosperity. I challenge you to ask yourself what these degrees really mean to your career.

An advanced college degree like an MBA or a Masters in Organizational Leadership must be the answer, right? Or is there something more?

Pairing my formal education with a bookshelf filled with countless books on leadership, management, success, and other business topics, it is safe to say I have read a lot of books about the subject of business. Eerily, I find many of them to be very similar. At times these titles begin to almost read as one continuous novel of regurgitated facts and opinion.

With all of the great programs on leadership offered in schools, written in books, and evangelized by speakers, some of my greatest leadership lessons have come from life. Here are five lessons in leadership that I would love to share with you.

- **Great leaders don't always do the right thing even when people are looking:** Part of being a leader is being human. While we have high expectations for those that lead us in our daily life, we have to realize that all our leaders (from our bosses, to community leaders, to our leaders in Congress) are flesh and blood. These people suffer from the same human condition as you and I. Mistakes will be made by everyone. The sooner you realize that fact, and the sooner you figure out how to learn from these mistakes, the more successful you will be. And, acknowledging the human factor will also make you a better leader

- **Leadership is very hard, even if it is innate:** It doesn't matter if you have been a leader from birth, or were promoted for the first time yesterday. Leading others is hard. You may someday read that somewhere, but however hard they tell you it is, multiply it by a large number, square it, and raise it to the Nth power. Okay, perhaps an exaggeration, but not by much. As a continuation of the point, you need to immediately realize that anytime you are dealing with other human beings, things will not be easy. When you become responsible for others in a leadership role, your objectives can seem nearly impossible. However, let me be the first (or insert actual number here: ___) to say that when you connect with your leadership abilities and make a difference for even a few teammates, the experience is incredibly rewarding.

- **You will never be able to lead everyone:** I have yet to come across more than a few humble (and quite successful) leaders that will admit they have struggled to lead certain people or personality types. You will find, throughout your personal and professional life that you cannot connect and lead everyone in every group. As a result, putting others on your team and surrounding yourself with great people is the key to success. If you find that you are a big picture leader, you may very well struggle with highly technical types that are very invested in the details. Guess what? Not a big deal, you just need to find someone that can empathize with that audience, but understands your passion. Then: delegate!

- **Your leadership style has to be you:** Nobody likes a phony. Check that, no one that I associate with likes or enjoys the company of a phony. And guess what, people don't follow others that they perceive as fake. Being genuine is vital to successful leadership. Focus on being real, being you, and leading people naturally from within. If you try to be someone you're not, or to emulate something you're not, people will take notice. When they do, it is often the end of any respect you have earned. That loss of respect and trust is a death sentence to an aspiring leader.

- **The real world doesn't value your education as much as you do:** Formal education is a great thing. As I mentioned previously, learning keeps the mind fresh. Education gives you an opportunity to better understand concepts and why they are important. What education doesn't do is build you a reputation of success, as a leader. Being a professor myself, I still feel the students are more interested in what I have accomplished outside of school than what I have done in the classroom.

Bottom line is: school is nice, but the real world will judge you on what you accomplish in your respective field. Whether that field is medical, technical... or maybe just being a wonderful parent

For me, the practical facts stopped me in my academic tracks, momentarily. I had to get the MBA to teach, but 99% of the value I bring is from what I do in the real world.

In academia, at times, the institution's bubble surrounds and protects you. It even makes you believe that the world may actually operate the way it does on campus.

In the books, everything sounds so clear-cut and easy; all you have to do are these 3 things and everyone will be mesmerized by your every word and you will become an instant peer to your industries greatest leaders. Unfortunately, it just doesn't work that way. The books and the school are meant to provide you context.

If you consider education as it was intended, it can be a great support tool as you adapt to your surroundings. I certainly recommend spending time in the classroom as a stepping-stone in self-development.

Formal education is not a road map for successful leadership. That kind of leadership has to start with you, your values, your knowledge, and all the other intangibles. Education is important, but true leadership starts with YOU.

EMBRACING YOUR DISSENTERS

DON'T YOU CRITICIZE ME!

It is inherent that we as human beings desire to be loved, supported, and appreciated.

While the support we seek certainly gives us a better sense of self, we must recognize that we are hardly flawless. Yet we often struggle to see our own imperfections.

One of the only ways for us to improve is to be aware of our shortcomings, and then choose to embrace them. But where does this awareness come from?

Ideally we recognize our own faults and then we work on them. This recognition is usually what drives us to fix our particular challenges.

However, often the best way to become aware is to listen to the feedback of others. People are often not hesitant to criticize. So, if you listen attentively, I assure you a whole dose of reality will come your way.

I've never met anyone who enjoys being criticized. It sort of goes against our nature, but nonetheless I just haven't come across the person that takes the whole "bring it on" approach to criticism.

I have seen some people who are pretty good on the surface at taking negative feedback (I'm one of them). However, deep down, we just don't like it.

This dislike of criticism is probably due to the fact that we as humans seek recognition (especially recognition from those closest to us). However, in the highly social world we live in, we seek the support of those closest to us – as well as those we barely even know.

Case in point: this past week I found out that someone I had done business with over seven years ago had a negative opinion about me; said I was cocky. I barely recall the interactions that I had with this person, but somehow seven years and several jobs later we crossed paths again and apparently I had left an unfavorable impression. For whatever reason the news of disapproval really bothered me.

In reality, I probably have a few people out there that aren't fond of me. I don't think this sentiment is the exception, but rather the rule. What is important is that we recognize reality, and use it to keep us humble.

As a leader (and a relatively outspoken one), there is no way that I can please everyone. I made the choice not to pursue universal approval many years ago, when I decided to move into a leadership role.

But I digress. The point here isn't to dissect the ways I have managed *not* to please everyone, but rather to share how to take a relatively negative means of communication and steer it toward a positive result.

As I heard about this transgression that led to the negative opinion (from what seems like forever ago), I realize that some of the errors in my ways were truly based on small (yet important) character flaws.

LEARNING FROM YOUR DISSENTERS

For as long as I have been in the business world, and in actuality as long as I have been alive I have been challenged by hubris. Early in my career it came across as an un-supported arrogance. As I moved into senior management roles in my early and mid-twenties, my hubris was sometimes just seen as absurd.

As I have grown throughout my career I have become more cognizant of my weaknesses including over-confidence. With this heightened awareness I have been able to take action to mitigate aspects of my personality, especially where it affects my ability to do my job well.

By no means have I been able to completely rid myself of hubris nor am I sure that I would want to. However, it has become more of a focus on taking the good that comes with self-confidence and eliminating the negative outcomes associated with arrogance.

Sometimes I have to remind myself that it takes a bit of hubris to make the tough calls. Those decisions that many choose not to make, or never have the opportunity to make, require a certain degree of self-assurance. When you rise to leadership roles, the tough decisions – made when your back is against the wall – that define you. At those tough times you have to believe in yourself, so a healthy confidence in oneself has to co-exist with the humility that makes great leaders.

Strangely, as I have grown older and more self-aware… the criticism has never stopped coming.

I had a mentor that used to say, "If you don't upset someone every day you probably aren't doing your job." While I don't know if that sage piece of advice was entirely true, what I did come away with from that quip is the following: the more you put yourself out there, the more likely you will draw criticism.

SORTING CONSTRUCTIVE FROM USELESS

I have no doubt that criticism does provide an opportunity for learning. But it is important that you see the difference between useful criticism and hateful banter.

While it is nice to always try to see the best in others (believe me, I try), some of the things that people hate most are the things that you may least suspect. For instance, people by nature are not always happy for you when you accomplish great things. The human condition often drives jealousy and disdain toward others that accomplish great things.

There is only one thing to be learned from those that choose jealous behavior, and that is to choose another behavior.

However, sometimes the feedback is useful, and when it is, be sure to take the chance to learn from it – even if you do have to admit weakness in the process.

While we all should try to accentuate our strengths, it never hurts to shore up a shortcoming or two in the pursuit of great results.

"As long as you challenge the status quo, you will be judged. The alternative is to be ignored." ~Unknown

26 A-Z CHARACTERISTICS OF A LEADER I'D LIKE TO FOLLOW

Tweet This:

Do you know what to look for in a leader? If you want to lead or be led, you better know what your followers are seeking in you.

While I'm not entirely certain there is such a thing as a "perfect" leader, I do sometimes try to think of what one may look like. If I had the chance to draw up the perfect leader from A-Z – a leader who I would want to follow – well, here's the list. With so many words to choose from, some of the letters were hard to choose, while others (like the letter "X") were hard to find even a single word.

Nevertheless, after boiling it down, the leader I would follow would definitely have these 26 characteristics. Where do you line up, on this list?

- **Available** – Always (within reason) there when they are needed.

- **Benevolent** – Intent is always a key. Good intent especially.

- **Charismatic** – During challenging times and great times this person inspires you to do your best.

- **Dreamer** – Any leader that I work for has to be a dreamer… Some call it vision, but it all starts with a dream!

- **Empathetic** – No matter what someone tells you, they want to feel understood. Any leader I would want to work for would know this, and operate this way.

- **Failure** – What? Yes, I believe any leader worth following has had some failures along the way. Now they are much more appreciative for their success.

- **Grateful** – To be great, you must be grateful. No one does it alone, ever!

- **Humble-** Being humble ranks among the most important of these. Arrogance is the shaky foundation for a leadership house of cards.

- **Inspirational** – I want a leader who aspires to inspire day in and day out.

- **Just** – As in guided by truth, reason, justice, and fairness.

- **Kind** – Nice guys do not finish last. People that allow themselves to be taken advantage of do. Not the same thing.

- **Level headed** – I call it ice water in the veins. If people see you get rattled they will pounce.

- **Mystique** – While I love transparency, I see mystique to a leader like swagger to a superstar. A little goes a long way.

- **Nimble** – Being able to quickly change the direction of the ship is key. There is a fine line between nimble and fickle. The former drives success, the latter drives you out of business.

- **Open Minded** – Nobody knows everything. Openness to others thoughts, ideas, and input is so important in a leader.

- **Positive** – Debbie Downer leads no one. I want a positive leader that balances positive with reality. But always focuses on the good and learns from the bad.

- **Quality** – A focus on quality over abundance is always a better path.

- **Reliable** – To be counted on to live their word.

- **Supportive** – This comes through feedback both positive and negative. But knowing the leader supports you gives you the confidence needed to persevere.

- **Transparent** – The ability to be open about plans and intent without creating fear and uncertainty is an art form mastered by the best leaders.

- **Unbiased** – Does not come with predisposition. Always learning and listening to form opinions based on the best information available.

- **Valor** – When the sky appears darkest, this person can be calm and courageous to continue to push forward.

- **Well Rounded** – Okay, it is 2 words, but I would always prefer to follow a person who has many dimensions to their life.

- **Xanadu** – In the journey of life this person seeks the "ideal" destination.

- **Yearning** – Having everything leaves nothing to shoot for. A little unfinished business makes for a great leader.

- **Zealous** – Everyone wants a leader that is devoted to the greater cause

If you could draw up the perfect leader A-Z what would you choose?

FIVE REASONS WHY YOUR MOTIVATION DOESN'T WORK

Tweet This:

It doesn't matter how dire YOUR situation is. To motivate the troops they have to believe in the vision. Don't lose sight of that.

I'm not exactly sure why or when it happened, but recently I have become enamored with the concept of motivation. I want to better understand why people do what they do and what makes them change their behavior.

As an always-aspiring-to-improve leader, like you, I thirst for knowledge in this subject area. I consistently look to my successes - and more appropriately, my failures - for ways to gain insight on the topic of motivation.

You will find that there are endless textbooks, blogs, white papers, and other sources of tireless theory on the subject of motivation. The experts will argue whether your motives are psychological, physiological, innate, emotional, behavioral, or some flavor of all of the above.

(Sigh – take a deep breath)

In the end, your motivation is probably some combination of all of the above. While the "catch all" answer may provide us some comfort, comfort is also what makes it so tricky for anyone attempting to motivate another human being.

Turns out that the effort to motivate is a combination of variables with each and every subject (person) in which we engage. Meaning that the uniqueness that we all strive for makes us increasingly difficult to properly motivate.

For the leader, motivation isn't as simple as they say. Perhaps rather than looking at every tip, tool, and trick to motivate, we can make some drastic improvements by just paying attention to what definitely doesn't work.

Let's examine five motivational pitfalls that can drastically diminish your leadership efforts.

- **Irrational/Self-Absorbed:** Most commonly seen by leaders that think their people are motivated by the leaders' need to accomplish something. While the "What's in it for me" philosophy still lives strong, it isn't motivational to many. Words like "me", "my", and "I" tend to create distance between people and the cause. Strong motivators understand the challenges with self-centered communication. They exemplify the opposite of "I – me – my" behavior, and they know engagement is imperative to get the most from their people. People simply want to feel a part of whatever they are doing. When they don't connect to the cause, the motivation and performance will lag behind as well.

- **Use of Fear and/or Coercion:** Do you think because you're the boss that people should just be fired up to do whatever you say? Perhaps a little tough love - or an occasional job security threat - is how you keep people inspired? Think again! People for the most part don't respond positively to the use of fear and coercion. In the enlightened society in which we live today people will take their fear and coercion and utilize it to motivate a change that you may not like... such as finding a new job (on your dime, while you're busy thinking about motivating them).

- **Inconsistent:** Are you a flavor of the day kind of person? I know that the proliferation of technology and the instantaneous nature of communication has led us to believe that our actions should yield instant results, but for the most part that isn't true. Consider the "Rule of Three" in business... everything takes three times as long, cost three times as much, and is three times as difficult. If you consider The Rule of Three, then why in the world would "motivation of the day" work for your team? You're driving the future for your businesses, not something you want to take lightly. The future is more than tomorrow's soup du jour.

- **Unrealistic:** I think one of the mistakes we make as people is how we tend to underestimate the intelligence of others. At times this underestimation can be subtle or even subconscious - and at other times, obtuse and offensive. People inherently tend to see when a goal is truly attainable. You may offer unbelievably lucrative incentives for someone trying to reach a goal, but if they don't see it as achievable, your offer is not only

101

demotivating, it's demeaning. People seek realistic goals, from leaders committed to attaining them. Are your goals realistic?

- **Irrelevant:** Previously, I mentioned the effect that our uniqueness has on motivation. We are all motivated by slightly different things. For example, I constantly discuss the importance of empathy as a key to successful leadership. Here is a perfect case where not understanding your people will lead you down a road to nowhere. Without empathy, you simply cannot motivate people – because you don't know what matters to them. (Remember how "don't know" is one of your greatest competitors?) While it isn't easy to brand every incentive or motivational strategy for everyone, you must consider what makes each person tick if you want your strategy to be relevant. And truly motivational.

Take a minute and think about how you motivate.

Do you bring out the best in people, or do you sometimes use tactics that aren't actually motivating at all? Being able to motivate and inspire is key to achieving just about anything in any facet of life. However, the way you go about it makes all the difference in the world.

SEVEN EVERYDAY WAYS TO INSPIRE YOUR EMPLOYEES

Tweet This:

Results come from employees that are motivated and inspired. Do you know how to keep them on track?

I call customers the "Life Blood" of any business. If this metaphor is correct, then our employees are the circulatory system.

Employees are involved in every aspect of the business. Therefore, they are generally involved in customer interaction. Having positive, engaged employees is going to be core to long-term success. And while this fact seems simple enough, a strong culture can be the difference between a poor business and a great one.

The happiest customers are often a byproduct of working with the happiest employees.

If keeping your customers inspired is the goal, you may be best served by focusing on your employees first. Some managers try to throw money at the employees, but reward (much like coercion) only works so well. And during tougher business times finding money isn't always easy (or possible).

Nevertheless, you must keep your team inspired.

So here are some ways (other than money) to create happier more effective employees.

- **Communicate** – More often than anything else, dissatisfied employees complain about a lack of communication. We all seek to understand, as human beings. As employees, we hope to know what is going on before our customers and suppliers. It is truly amazing how bad some leaders and managers are at "surprises" for the team. Try over-communicating a little bit. Trust me, they will let you know when you are sharing too much.

- **Vision** – In addition to the communication strategy, leadership has to show a sense of vision. Many of the happiest employees work for companies where they feel there is a clear sense of direction. Therefore these team members know what their work is making a contribution. A lot of companies write a mission and/or vision statement, and then don't look at it again for years. Yes, vision is part of the business planning process, but more importantly, vision is part of the every day. Share your vision, and get your employees invested in your vision. They will perform at a noticeably higher level.

- **Presence** - Leadership doesn't happen only in the corner office. Some strategy texts have identified a term

MBWA (Management by Walking Around). While it sounds kind of silly, employees seek to see their leadership involved and engaged. Getting out with the teams - in the office and in the field - will show them just how much you care. Doesn't have to be every day, but your appearance should be often enough that they know you are connected. Do your employees consider you engaged?

- **Take Notice** – If the annual review is the only time that you let your employees know how they are doing, then you are sorely missing the mark. Some HR thought leaders have even suggested eliminating the annual review. Employees want and require constant feedback. The goal with feedback isn't to babysit; the goal is to make sure resources stay aligned with the long and short term goals. Alignment is far more likely to happen with regular feedback. Sometimes even the smallest feedback can generate a great response from an employee.

- **Little Things** – Perhaps big bonuses, raises, and trips aren't in the budget. But how about taking the sales team out for a burger and a beer after work? Too often, leadership thinks that if they can't give a big raise to the team that there is no point in doing anything. Training opportunities, trade shows, and other small things can be quite inspiring to an employee.

- **New Opportunities** – Employees also yearn for continued growth and development. As an employer, giving additional responsibility to a hard working employee can be quite rewarding for both parties. While a promotion may require substantial payout, sometimes that bridge can be gapped slowly and when the up and coming employee is generating new improved company results the compensation can follow. Nevertheless, employees seek mobility. Most small organizations lack the formal growth structure of larger enterprises. A little creativity can go a long way here.

- **Positivity** – There is probably nothing more demoralizing for an employee than a leader that walks around moping and pouting. Whatever your current positivity level is, amp it up a notch. Keep it genuine and stick with a sense of realism, but even during tough times keep your head up. Employees look to leadership for stability. If you show this stability they will feel more able to focus on what you need them to be doing...generating results!

- **Communicate** – This one is so important that I felt compelled to say it twice. No matter what else you focus on, if you communicate more effectively you will have happier, more inspired employees.

If it is inspired customers you seek, then start by giving your team a lift....

How else do you inspire your employees?

SECTION II:
SOCIAL SAVVY

YOUR SOCIAL VOICE:
ARE YOU A FAKER?

Tweet This:

We all need to be adaptable, but being fake should never be part of your repertoire.

From the time that I was young I can remember my mother's "Phone Voice."

The metaphor of her "Phone Voice" is how I define the way she answers the phone. Her greeting was like no other I'd ever heard; comprised of the clearest, kindest, most eloquent voice. It was unmistakable. It didn't really matter what was going on around her. She always answered this way.

I distinctly remember one time when she was screaming her head off at my sister and me only for her to stop when the phone rang to deliver a perfect rendition of her famous greeting.

While my mother is a wonderful person, this voice was not really her. It was a total fraud. I knew this even as a child because she never spoke with this voice - except when she picked up a call.

Since my not-so-fond memories of this date back to before the days of caller ID, I'm pretty sure she created "Phone Voice" just in case someone really important was calling.

Now that we always know who is calling, the element of surprise is gone. This knowledge (also called Caller ID) allows even her to answer the phone a bit more candidly.

The funny thing is how small things in life can have a big impact. The fake voice that my mother used to answer the phone drove me crazy. I never understood why you would want to be anyone but you, and because of this I swore I would only be me. I never wanted anyone to question if I'm real.

Today the phone voice has waned, but it has been replaced. This time, not by good old mom, but by a mass of social media users who speak in "phone voice". Or is that "phony voice"?

This mass of users is best characterized by those who display an image, instead of an authentic persona…because of the uncertainty of who may be listening.

After all, a good first impression is important.

Problem is that there are some misconceptions about the good ol' first impression.

If you have to lie, mislead, misinform, or act any way that isn't representative of "YOU," then it isn't a good first impression. Your first impression is the foundation of a relationship that will have to continue to be built on false pretenses.

Unfortunately, the real "you" always finds its way to the surface; it's really only a matter of time until that happens.

As I have been around the "Social Media" world longer, I have become more and more aware of the fake voice online.

It isn't really that hard to see it. Just think about your 360 degree life away from the internet. People just aren't so one dimensional in real life, but they can often seem that way online. Overly happy, nice, affectionate (hugs, xo, etc.), inspirational or other...

This twisted dimension can become even more visible when you start to meet some of these "Handles" in the real world. Instantly, it's clear that the online personality and the offline person are hardly one and the same.

What is even crazier is sometimes I end up liking the real person better. That affinity is probably because no one is happy, perfect or shiny all of the time.

This ebb and flow of life often leaves me wondering: why so many fakers?

Obviously not everyone is faking it. I've met some truly wonderful people via the social sphere. Would it surprise you if I suggest that many of the best ones are often much more electric in person than on line?

Having said that, I have also met some of the most prolific people online to find out that they are hardly prolific in real life.

As for me, I am what I am. This fact will probably limit my potential in the social space, but I'm okay with that. I've always believed in having a few really meaningful relationships rather than lots of acquaintances.

You can also count on the fact that I'm going to share what I think. This is the only thing that makes sense to me since Social Media is really just the interaction of "Real People" on a virtual platform. But I digress...

So how about you? Are you for real, or are you doing social media with a phone voice?

WHEN DID ADVERTISING BECOME SOCIAL MEDIA?

Tweet This:

Even disguised as well intended, spam is spam. Always a no-no.

BUY FROM ME!!!

It feels like everyone in the social universe has something for sale.

- Attend my Twitter Chat
- Subscribe to my blog
- Purchase my book
- Like my Facebook page

While I am certain (certainly cynical) that every one of these chats, blogs, books, and pages are the single most informative, game-changing and life-altering ways that a person could spend their time, I am beginning to question when Social Media platforms turned into other more intrusive marketing methods.

May I ask: when is it appropriate to revisit the rules of professional selling …or perhaps just civility?

SOCIAL MEDIA ISN'T ADVERTISING... IS IT?

Over the past few months as more and more companies and sole proprietors have embraced social as a method for customer acquisition, I have seen an escalating trend of companies mistaking social platforms for (unpaid) advertising.

- Tweets linked to "Buy My...Whatever it is I'm selling."

- DM's to every new follower with a hard close (Following you doesn't directly correlate with the fact that we want to buy whatever you are selling, it is more of a "hey, we'd like to know more")

- Linked In messages with a "Deal" for something you didn't ask for.

With this proverbial flurry of fire-bombs trying to sell your me-too service, book, or gadget, the Social Universe is becoming increasingly like the coupon section of the Sunday paper. The biggest difference is that people went to the ads section of the Sunday paper on purpose. Now we go to a social platform to share and communicate, only to be bombarded with spam.

If Social Media and Advertising were the same thing then wouldn't they have just called it Advertising?

YES: THE LAW OF AVERAGES, BUT NOT DIRECT MARKETING

Even today direct mail from my favorite retailers as well as complete unknowns still shows up in the mailbox. Similar electronic versions flood my email as well. Now this mailing method has invaded social.

While it may not get full attribution rights, it seems that direct mail may have something to do with the "Hit 'Em All" approach that we see in the social sphere.

Somewhere along the line, it was decided by many Social Marketers that if we just send a flyer to everyone (Tweet, FB Request, LI Message) then we should get some level of conversion. The law of averages absolutely rings true in sales and marketing. After all you won't ever get a sale that you don't ask for. However, if your method of selling is purely spamming every person that you come in contact with, you will never be more than a spammer.

SELLING WITHOUT TRUST

What strikes me as even more ironic is the amount of spammy selling being performed by self-proclaimed gurus. These sales and marketing experts promise to show you the way to sales success and enlightenment.

If I were to attend a sales conference, and the expert told me that my first move is to walk into the prospect's office and plop a contract on their desk, I would be alarmed.

Anyone that has carried a bag knows that you can't just walk up to people on the street and ask them to buy from you and expect any level of success. A sale (tangible or intangible) always begins with a relationship, which leads to a level of trust, which ultimately leads to the discovery of an opportunity to engage in a transaction of equal benefit for all parties involved.

QUIT THROWING UP ON ME

Nobody goes on Twitter looking to buy your e-book. Even if I was to follow you or like something you shared, it is hardly me saying "Yes, please! Let me have what you are selling." Rather it is me saying, "Okay, you appear to be interesting. Allow me to find out more." Further it would generally be preferred that I can learn more without massive intrusion into my life.

People are savvy consumers. While they probably won't find you if they don't know they are looking for you, the true objective online is to build bridges that create roadways that lead to open doors (network).

Unfortunately if your version of networking is merely throwing up your pitch on anyone that you think may be listening (they probably are not) then you most likely are going to struggle to get introductions... let alone sales.

WHAT SHOULD WE DO?

Success will and should be recognized differently by everyone. However, I do recommend a return to the more human side of selling and engagement.

Sales - on any platform- has rules. The first of those rules is that without trust, there is very little chance a sale will take place. If what you are selling is more than a mere commodity, then the approach must be built to match.

Try to imagine a real, in-person engagement. If you wouldn't approach the in-person sale the way you are doing it in Social Media, then you may be doing it wrong.

If marketing is your goal, then know your channels. Social is the information sharing and engagement channel that lives in cooperation (and sometimes disdain) with advertising. Being on the social networks allows you a chance to obtain real feedback from real customers via real interaction. So make sure that the efforts put into these networks enables this rather than alienates those that may be interested in your offering.

While I stand by my belief that there is no one right way to do "Social," I do believe there are some wrong ways. Let's keep Social about learning, sharing, and engaging, and leave the spam and advertising where they belong... elsewhere.

SOCIAL MEDIA FOR THE C SUITE:
ARE YOU A CE "NO" OR A CE "GO"?

Tweet This:

Being Social isn't only for the birds. It is for CEO's as well.

TWITTER SUCKED – OR SO I THOUGHT…

The first few days I went on Twitter I was hardly impressed. In fact, I thought these tweets just plain stunk. I signed up, followed a few stars and people that I knew, and then I watched the "stream." My first impression was that it was total nonsense. I saw it as a social experiment (gone bad) where you could find celebrities promoting, media outlets broadcasting, children chatting, and professionals bantering. Why would anyone waste time with this garbage?

At this point I didn't have a following, or even a sense of what was happening. The whole thing seemed pointless, and I was totally lost. After a few weeks of watching passively, I came to realize two things. First, I am really bad at Twitter, and second, I now had more questions than answers.

A few of the questions that crossed my mind were…

- What are all of these people doing here?

- Who is reading their tweets?

- Why do some people have so many followers and others so few?

- Is this just a massive waste of time?

- How can I possibly use this to improve our business?

I suppose I shouldn't have been surprised about my early impressions of Twitter. It was nothing more than curiosity that led me to finally sign up (Curiosity? Almost cynicism, really). I couldn't watch a television show, visit a restaurant, or surf the web without hearing about Twitter. I had to see for myself. My opinion was that Twitter was nothing more than a place for celebrities to say regrettable things, and perhaps some type of popularity contest for the rest of the world. What I believed that I knew for sure was that social media was nothing more than a giant waste of time for a C-Level executive (like me).

SOCIAL MEDIA: HYPE, WHAT HYPE?

I often proclaim to be a social media newbie. However, I must confess that prior to joining Twitter, I had been on LinkedIn for a period of time, but essentially I used it as nothing more than an electronic Rolodex finding minimal value in that. Beyond that, our company had a Twitter handle (near dormant) and a Facebook page (completely dormant).

Truth be told, I just thought that Social Media was hype. I saw it as a circus of flying rhetoric with no meaning that served as nothing more than a waste of time for both myself and my organization. I viewed it as a PR/Marketing thing, primarily for large B2C companies, and most certainly not a place for a B2B.

PERSISTENCE PAYS OFF

It would have been really easy to have gone dark. Why not close my account, and disappear from Twitter (and the hype) - only to be seen again by real humans, with real needs. No more screaming into a dark cave and hoping that somehow someone would hear me. I wasn't used to being ignored, and that was what Twitter felt like to me.

The caveat that kept me going is that I'm a fierce competitor (a blessing and a curse). I don't like to lose at anything. (If you don't believe me, come watch me play Wii with my kids. Losing is not an option) There had to be something more to Twitter - and a reason that all of these people were spending so much of their time there. I was determined to figure it out.

Over the next several months I continued exploring the dynamic Twitter landscape. I committed to engaging, connecting, and getting involved with dynamic individuals. I read blogs about success on Twitter, social media etiquette. More than anything else I paid attention to how others used Twitter to enhance their business and individual brand. I created my own crash course in networking in the digital world. I learned a lot, and it paid off!

THE RESULTS ARE IN

I will proudly tell the C-Level community that Social Media is no longer something to consider, it is something that you must engage in. As the face of your respective companies, Social Media aligns in so many ways with your position. Here are a few of those ways.

- **Branding** – As a C level leader you are responsible for (and often interchangeable with) the branding, image, and awareness of the organization. Social Media provides a conduit to brand both yourself and your organization to a wide audience. The larger you grow the audience, more people aware of your value.

- **Networking** – As a CEO or other C suite executive, you bring tremendous value to your organization when you build a strong professional network. It is amazing how many CEO's and other senior executives you can find and connect with on Twitter. CEO to CEO engagement can lead to some tremendous deals, and can move them along quickly. (Tweet me @MillennialCEO for details)

- **Thought Leadership** – Executives should (but often don't) work to establish a reputation as thought leaders in their respective fields, communities, and networks. By providing thought-provoking content, and establishing your knowledge in your field, you can become visible to thousands (if not more) of potential buyers. Even better, you can indirectly lead a team of word of mouth marketers for your product or service.

- **Engagement** – Social Media has created a human condition that makes almost everyone accessible. If you are seen as an elitist, your brand may suffer. By being accessible, engaging, and humble on Social Media, you can build trust with your audience. I have found most people are more than willing to engage, and those engagements have led to incredibly meaningful business relationships (and a few friendships).

- **Mentorship** - There are many executives doing a great job of using Twitter for their companies, and for their individual brand. I suggest you find a few that you feel are doing a great job and watch their contribution. If you can engage these thought leaders, perhaps they can mentor you more directly. I had a few great mentors on Twitter that completely changed the experience for me.

PARTICIPATION – WHAT IT'S ALL ABOUT

In the time I have been actively *participating* on Twitter, I have built countless great relationships, expanded awareness of my organization, our goals, our direction, and what it is that makes us great.

If you are a senior executive still sitting on the Social Media sidelines, I have one piece of advice.

Social Media will provide a return that is very much in line with what you put into it. Signing up and creating a profile will probably provide no tangible return. Similar to joining a new networking group or trade organization, building relationships often takes time. However, if you participate, and commit to your message and your value (both organization and individual), there is likely an audience willing and ready to help spread your message.

So jump on in and get started. I assure you won't regret it! Here are a few suggestions to make your online experience more meaningful.

Many of these tips will be driven from personal experience. Hopefully this shortens the learning curve for senior level managers looking to maximize the Social Media Experience.

Tip #1: Listen – Probably a fundamental tool that helped you reach the level you are at in business today. Many C–Level executives are used to being listened to and immediately respected. Places like Twitter are have hundreds of millions of users, many of whom have figured out how to use the medium very successfully. By listening, especially to those who have become most successful in the Social Media space, you can quickly learn how to use it as a conduit for networking and brand development.

A specific recommendation I have for listening is to search for counterparts, competitors, and supply chain partners. Watch and listen to how they are using Social Media.

Tip #2: Share – Please note that Sharing is not "Broadcasting." I strongly discourage broadcasting in Social Media unless you have a tremendous audience of highly engaged followers whom are hanging on your every word. When I suggest sharing, I am talking about industry best practices, relevant articles, blogs you have written, or other content that helps others interested in your business type/industry. If people find the content that you provide to be meaningful and interesting, you will quickly grow your following.

One way to share to your target audience is to create content. My recommendation is writing a blog or creating video blogs that establish you as a thought leader in your respective industry.

SOCIAL MEDIA BUZZWORDS HAVE LOST THEIR WAY

Tweet This:

In the boardroom and the internet, buzzwords are a great way to sound smart while saying very little.

Social Media – it's the Wild, Wild West of media platforms as well as the future for how we will all communicate. I'm waving at your email... you are going bye-bye (premonition free of charge – email is becoming a thing of the past!)

Social Media is also a place where people who have never historically had an audience can find an audience. This audience can be found in many ways, but primarily through a guerilla approach where a tremendous amount of time is spent on the Social Platforms. The size of the audience can be expanded by employing strategies such as curating great content, creating better content, and of course by sucking up to important people.

If those tactics don't reflect your strategy, you can implement begin by writing blogs about the hottest new shiny object. Not too long ago it was Klout, before that it

124

was Triberr, and most recently it has been Pinterest. What is it today, as you read these words?

If the shiny object strategy doesn't get you where you want to go, you can play Social Media Buzzword bingo. Throwing out buzzwords in the Social Stream is sure to get you "Liked," and loved.

However, I'm calling it out now:

Some of these buzzwords have lost their meaning... and perhaps their soul.

I want to be clear that I believe many of these words started with good intentions, and with proper application they can still have meaning in limited context. But much like the business buzzwords, it is man-made sputrid that causes folks to lose their way. (Wonder what sputrid is? That's a word I made up to define the nonsense that comes from today's pseudo-experts).

In no particular order, here are 5 Social Media buzzwords that were well intended but have lost their way...

- **Engagement:** The idea of making a strong connection between people or between a person and a brand. More than just simply communicating, we are seeking to engage our audiences. Given that most of us have an attention span of about 4 nanoseconds on the social platforms, I would say most of us aren't as engaged as we like to claim.

- **Authenticity:** I could write about this for days. I have met many people whom I've first connected with via various Social Platforms. I would say at least half of the time, I find the people to be nothing like their "Social Personality." There is a big difference between acting authentic and being authentic.

- **Reciprocity:** We are all supposed to reciprocate. This universal task was decided by the pundits of Social Media. Some folks reciprocate very well, but most of the people who preach the behavior hardly follow it. If reciprocating means sharing of five of your best friends and five people who you worship, then I retract the aforementioned comments. However it doesn't, so I don't.

- **Influence:** I blame and credit Klout for making this word relevant and then for destroying it. The idea of having influence has SO MANY variables that your Twitter stream and Facebook likes can only tell a fraction of the story. Yet people want to put a score on you that defines how influential you are? PLEASE!

- **Community:** I really want to thank everyone in this great *community* (sarcasm) who reads my book. (Seriously, I genuinely do appreciate everyone who takes the time to read my book. And I hope you tell your friends, so they will read it too!) However, the average reader doesn't just read a few blogs and associate with a few brands. There is a plethora of information, online and in print, and connecting with a brand or a message is not the same as joining a community. Association is not community when it comes to brands. Community as in family, business, neighborhood, church, etc… Those things are community. And yes, in some cases we can create online communities. Facebook, Twitter and LinkedIn are three examples. After that, the community is readers, subscribers, and, if I'm lucky, friends and acquaintances. But believe me, there's room for more in this community and it would be great if we could continue the connection online (http://millennialceo.com is a good place to start).

THE DEATH OF DISTANCE:
SOCIAL MEDIA AND COLLABORATION

Tweet This:

The future will yield a very different type of work place. We are closer together than ever. Welcome to the connected world!

It has become difficult to remember back to when you didn't know everything about everyone in your life at any given moment.

You know those times where you would meet up with a friend for coffee, or perhaps some distant relatives, just to see what was going on?

Fast forward to today.

The whole world is on Facebook, so we keep up with each other's personal lives that way. We of course are LinkedIn to one another so we know what the professional skinny is, and beyond those platforms we are tweeting, pinning, Klouting, and stumbling all over one another.

When we do want to engage, we have platforms for that. The Social Platforms above have created a nice medium for the quick interaction, either via a posting or using an embedded messaging tool. If we want to take engagement one step further, platforms like Skype, Google and Facebook will allow us to jump on a video chat.

In the enterprise, you have businesses utilizing technologies such as Cisco Unified Communications and Microsoft Office Communicator to do full collaboration - bringing the workforce closer together regardless of distance. Virtually one button from phone to video to email to text means we are almost always connected.

Life's compartments (family, personal, work) have become inseparable. Collaboration has become truly immersive. What once could only be imagined is now done with greater ease than picking up the phone and making a call.

In reality communication has reached a point where we don't really need to ask one another how we are doing, we just need to hit the interwebs - because all of the information can be found right there. To some extent, social media and collaboration tools have facilitated the drive-by "How you doing?"

If you don't know what the "Drive-By" is, it is what I refer to when someone in the hall passed you by, made eye contact, and asked you, "How you doing?"

While they did ask you the question, far more often than not they actually had no interest in hearing the answer.

So what does this all mean?

It is official… DISTANCE IS DEAD (So is most of your privacy by the way – an issue for a later time).

Recently I was lecturing to one of my International Marketing Classes about how we communicate in the workplace. I asked the class of senior-level business students about their preferred method of communication.

(Many of these students are already in the professional workforce, or are just about to enter it).

Nearly everyone's preferred method was text message, followed closely by social media. These MBA students told me they respond to voice mail with email, and email with text messages.

Moreover, they are seeking the platform that brings the most immediacy - with the *least* interpersonal interaction.

While most of us have accepted the various social platforms, both in our personal and professional lives, many of us still view social media as a silo that is separate from our more intimate communications.

We may not regularly break bread with the majority of our friends on Twitter, we certainly engage them via the content we share, in the moment soon after.

The context of communication has almost reached the point in which we know more about virtual strangers than we could ever hoped for. (Or ever wanted to?)

The abundance of knowledge is powerful, and it serves as a gateway to better interpersonal relationships, better business, and better communications. However, this knowledge does have a price. If we aren't careful, TMI (Too much information) will allow us to become so busy being social that we no longer truly communicate.

Interpersonal becomes replaced by "Internet Personal." Moreover, our relationships are becoming replaced by a scanning of online updates, profiles, blogs, and information - keeping us up to date, without ever really speaking.

Those that will be most successful with technology and innovation will leverage the "Death of Distance." Managing the risks, these leaders will use new communication tools to stay informed *and* stay in touch.

The Death of Distance is an opportunity for all to better collaborate, communicate, and innovate - through whatever opportunities and challenges that life brings next. To unlock the full potential of The Death of Distance, communication tools must be used appropriately - rather than as a replacement for more intimate interaction.

In time, our connections will only get better, faster… and with higher definition. The Death of Distance is bringing us closer than ever before.

Wondering… Can I look forward to seeing and hearing from you soon… or will you just be following from afar?

STOP COUNTING FOLLOWERS, START BUILDING RELATIONSHIPS

Tweet This:

It is easy to get caught up in the numbers. But focus on the numbers that count.

A LOT OF NUMBERS – LITTLE CONTEXT

The whole social media spectrum is rampant with analytics. No matter what Social Media outlet you are utilizing, you will find metrics around every corner screaming in your ear to get your attention.

For example…

- How many Twitter Followers do you have?
- How many Facebook Friends?
- How many times are you circled on Google+?
- What is your Klout / Kred Score?
- How many times has your Page been "Liked?"
- How many Blog Subscribers do you have?

Sadly, the above serve as just a few examples of the metrics game. I could actually go on and on with the inordinate number of data points that exist in the social space. However, I'm going to move in another direction.

Data + Context = Information

In the world of marketing and media, metrics matter. Numbers are the best way to measure ROI. Therefore, it is important that we know how many eyeballs are seeing our work.

The problem is the data, in itself, is often raw.

For instance: you are brand "X", and you pay $3 million for a Super Bowl ad. Five million people watch the commercial. How many dollars in revenue did you just create?

Answer: You and they (the marketing wizards) really have no idea.

Further, even if someone sees a Doritos commercial and then goes out and purchases a bag of Doritos, what is to say that purchase wouldn't have happened anyway?

Reality: There are simply too many variables.

LET'S TAKE A STEP BACK: BRAND Y-O-U

Major brands have purpose in their media campaigns and commercials, beyond just creating revenue. Corporate brands are attempting to stay front of mind by staying in front of the consumer. In many ways, companies are building relationships via traditional media - entirely possible when you have massive budgets for air time.

However, most of us in the Social Media realm are not major brands. Does this describe you? You do not have endless budgets, and the brand that you are most appropriately representing is yourself. In other words, not Brand X – Brand Y-O-U.

If personal branding is the case (And I believe that, at some level, it's always the case!) then the measurements we use need to be different than Brand X.

HOW MANY FOLLOWERS DO YOU HAVE?

When I talk to someone that isn't a big Social Media user, the conversation is sort of funny to me. They ask about follower counts, and when I say I have 78,000 or so (on Twitter as I write this), they are blown away. If you ask a Twitter veteran the same question they would say that 78,000 is nothing.

I know dozens of people with north of 100,000 Twitter followers. While those are huge numbers, what does that size of following really mean?

Given the fact that followers can be easily purchased for about a penny a piece, as can likes and most other Social Metrics, I'm beginning to think that the numbers in themselves don't mean all that much.

Followers can be gained through follow-back tools and metrics, and the system can be gamed through "Like This" tactics, where someone has to like a page in order to gain access to content that they originally sought out.

Perhaps that system sheds some light on how someone with 100,000, 200,000 or even 500,000 followers may share something of yours ... and it doesn't receive a single RT.

None of this is to say that great metrics don't mean great things. The message is that the numbers (by themselves) require context. Context matters. Great numbers only mean great results if numbers are all that are being sought.

Which for most of us isn't the case.

WHY AM I HERE?

The other day someone asked me what all the Tweeting had translated to in terms of business success. It was a great question that stopped me in my tracks.

I hadn't joined Twitter to close business or really to sell anything, really. It was my desire to connect with people, information, and ideas that would foster continued growth for me as an individual.

As I mentioned before, I had always thought that perhaps someday Twitter would amount to something tangible, but I have never directly sought that.

Perhaps I am naive, but I'm online to build relationships.

For me, social media is a qualitative effort that cannot be measured by followers, friends, Klout, pins, +1′ s, or any other quantifiable metric.

I believe the value that can come out of just a few really meaningful relationships will greatly supersede the value of a massive following – a following that is mostly disconnected, or distracted, or both.

Test This Theory: What percentage of your Followers do you speak to regularly (more than 1x a week or month for that matter).

WHY ARE YOU HERE?

Social Media is different for everyone. Everyone has a purpose, even if you don't know what it is.

Nevertheless, if your purpose is just adding numbers then you can count on just average results.

I liken the accumulation of large metrics with buying nice things to impress your neighbors. AKA, "Keeping up with the Joneses"

When I grew up my father used to say this to me about the subject of the mythical "Joneses"…

"People buy things they don't need, with money they don't have, to impress people that don't care."

In Social Media I re-purpose this to say, "People collect followers they don't need, to accumulate numbers that mean nothing, so they can impress people they don't know."

Greatness is built in both the width and the depth of the connections we have. So why are you online? What do you hope to gain, from social media? And, is your strategy effective in promoting Brand Y-O-U, through real connections?

DOES SOCIAL SHARING EQUAL PUBLIC ENDORSEMENT?

Tweet This:

Online and Offline, everything you say has repercussions. Try and make them positive, so share carefully.

For whatever reason, I have long had disdain for the Social Media users that put the all-encompassing quote "Views are my own" within their various social bios/profiles.

Not because I don't believe that the views are their own, but rather the subtlety (Is it all that subtle?) by which they are saying that they are excusing their respective organization from anything stupid they may say or do. The problem is, the world doesn't work that way. What you do outside of work or on social platforms ultimately is a reflection on all of the communities in which you participate; your workplace being one of them. Remember Brand Y-O-U?

I have long stood by the motto that I will judge (subconsciously of course) your various affiliations by the matter in which you tweet, share, or blog. Judgment like that may not be fair, but neither is life.

Those that say they don't judge your online presence are probably lying to you or to themselves. So, if you go out and make a fool of yourself on your own time, and you later lose your job for it, I won't feel bad for you.

When you are sharing online, caution should be drawn because whether you like it or not, your stakeholders are being judged by your actions.

With this impact in mind, curate and share carefully because everything you say (or post) leaves a footprint in the sands of time.

Want to know more? Well, I have a confession to make.

I don't read everything I share.

I read a lot of it, I skim some of it, and sometimes I just pass it along.

Now before you judge me, hold on. I can't be the only sane person in the world that does this. With the amount of content that goes out on the interwebs and the gross number of shares that certain sites get, I have a hard time believing that everyone reads every single article. (I think somewhere I can actually hear the silent gasp of a social media purist.)

I have a plan and I have purpose. So I share my ideas, with you in mind.

It seems that we have come to a bit of a crossroads here. With so much content and so many communities, how do we decide what to share? Further, how should we appropriately explain the demarcation between sharing content, and that of a public endorsement?

SHARING IS CARING

As we have all built up our social communities, we have set some expectations as to how we engage and share. Some of us are more conversational and chatty, while others are much more content based. In some cases this pendulum swings depending on work volume, time of day/year, or just the ever-changing commitments that we have.

I have built a tight knit community around subjects such as leadership, marketing, and technology and there is a tremendous amount of reciprocity within my community. I have hundreds of members in my Triberr community, as well as many others whom I reciprocate via guest blogs or other sharing mechanisms. (Not familiar with Triberr? Check it out right here: http://triberr.com)

For the most part, my connections all write good content. As a result I have no issue sharing it within my communities. Having said that, I don't in all cases agree with the content. In some cases I don't agree at all.

BUT IS A SHARE AN ENDORSEMENT?

If we are all judged based upon the actions we take online, then a share could be misconstrued for an endorsement.

Why in the world would anyone share something that they don't like or agree with, right?

Truth be told, the majority of what I share I at least agree with *for intent*. Some of the content is interesting, provocative, or different - and worth reading. Some portion of the shared content I may disagree with, but still think it is worth a read.

I don't necessarily endorse everything that I share. However, am I responsible to point that out? If I share something - whether marketing focused or politically charged - does that mean I side with the article? Whether I agree or not, am I endorsing the author, or the viewpoint, or all of the above?

Does the tweeting of a Huffington Post article make me a liberal? Does the LinkedIn share of a Fox News report make me a staunch conservative?

Personally, the share means it is interesting to me and I think it might be of value to you. Or, perhaps that latest share is content from someone that I respect. Generally speaking, an endorsement is only if I say specifically that I agree – check the comments on the post to find out!

ON THE OTHER HAND...

Why does social sharing have to be called out as "an endorsement" before it counts?

The fact is that there are always two sides of the coin, so we can't neglect the fact that sometimes we will be unfairly associated with the content we share. Keep that in mind when making the decision on the content that you curate. Remember how I said life wasn't always fair?

SO IS SHARING AN ENDORSEMENT, OR ISN'T IT?

Unfortunately, like so many things in life, the answer here isn't going to be black and white. It is going to come with shades of grey. The fact is with so many eyeballs on everything we do these days we will be constantly judged.

So the more important question is: who are you trying to reach with your message and your impressions?

For instance, if you are a business owner and you work for yourself (and your customers, of course) you may not be opposed to sharing a lot of diverse content - with a small risk of offending someone along the way. However, if you have a high profile corporate job you may want to be very careful what you put into the social sphere, and where your content comes from.

The other big focus should be on your community. I have long heard an expression that you cannot fly with the eagles if you are hanging with the turkeys. I suggest thinking of your community in a similar way.

If the majority of the people in your social media circles are people of high moral standards, and they put out a good product, you can generally be sure that sharing their content comes with low risk. If the source is known for good content, then you are generally safe as well. I find articles from Mashable, TechCrunch, and Harvard Business Review (for instance) to generally be pretty safe. The problem with only sharing from those sites is that you and every other person that knows how to tweet shares that content.

The only way to be 100% certain to never offend is to curate everything thoroughly. Read the post, check the links, and then add your input when sharing, to make sure you safely and effectively present your view.

If I had the time to do so, I would. But I would be lucky to share 2 things a day if I had to read everything - which would probably not make me all that interesting to follow or engage.

Nevertheless, share carefully my friends...

FOUR SOCIAL MEDIA PERSONALITIES TO AVOID

Tweet This:

If your time is a precious asset then you have to avoid the noise that is trying to waste it.

For the most part being social is not a spectator sport. However, if you spend a little time online you find yourself doing more spectating than you might think. In social media, conversations are happening all around us. Sometimes we join in, but other times we just watch. When you watch long enough, you begin to see things that you might not like.

Fortunately in Social communities there are millions of users, so you can steer away from what you don't like and focus on what you do. After all, you wouldn't hang out in person with someone you don't care for - so do that online.

As a student of people and a person that always seeks to be happy, I have taken notice of some online personalities that make my online experience less tolerable.

Here are 4 of the worst social media culprits, and why I avoid them.

1. **"The Over-Sharer"**- This person feels compelled to share every accomplishment, conversation, thought and activity that they encounter. Morning, noon, and night they are keeping you informed of their every move. Every once in a while they drop something into the stream everyone cares to see, but usually... not so much. This personality is why sites like "Lamebook" were created. Thankfully, these individuals share so much with so many people that their follies become our funnies. Is there ever a point where the person who shares too much realizes, "I think I share too much?" I say no, and they prove it every day.

2. **"Internet Muscles"**- Behind their keyboard, this personality believes they are the Incredible Hulk. They feel like they can say anything they want - to anyone - and there will be no repercussions. I understand the feeling of safety that people have hiding in their basement behind an alias, but I also find this particular personality to be so toxic and destructive within any community that they choose to join.

3. **"The I-Hole"**- The I-Hole is actually just an internet A-Hole. This personality thinks anyone who disagrees with them to be one or more of these "I" words: Ignorant, Incompetent, or Insolent. This person is completely incapable of reasoning, compromise, or even having a productive debate. It takes a maximum of 2 conversations regarding a challenging premise to identify this character. Unfortunately, there are no known antidotes, except the "hide" button.

4. **"Like Me, Like Me Guy"**- Would you really walk up to every person you meet on the street and ask them to Like your Facebook Page? On Twitter, Facebook, and every other Social platform you are bombarded with beggars asking for likes, follows, and shares. You wouldn't do that to someone in real life, so why do you do it online, Like Me, Like Me Guy? These people aren't really doing any damage; they are just SO ANNOYING. You will never win friends, influence people, or even keep followers if you constantly beg to be Liked.

While there are different strokes for different folks, I strongly suggest avoiding these types for a better Social Media Experience.

SECTION III: OPERATIONS

CORPORATE CULTURE:
A BUSINESS GAME CHANGER

Tweet This:

If you don't have control of the culture, you will be amazed how hard it is to get anything done.

For ages, the pundits, educators, and practitioners have sought relentlessly to figure out what it is that leads some businesses to successful outcomes while others stagnate, sway, or die.

From afar, two businesses can look, feel, and act very similar.

They may be in a similar industry, create similar products/services, and even be located in the same geographic region. However, with all of these similarities, it isn't uncommon to see one company thrive while the other can barely survive.

With so much in common, the idea that similar looking businesses can yield vastly different results seems crazy. At least on the surface...

The subtleties start with the origination of the business, but the great differentiator comes from what all businesses have in common... People.

Businesses are built on ideas. They blossom around their strategy and thrive on execution. When and if they succeed, they succeed because of their people.

The collective power of the people, the success, processes and hard work is something we refer to as "Corporate Culture." Culture is at the heart of every business - and may be the most important indicator of whether or not a company will succeed. Yet culture is discussed far too rarely and worked on even less. This lack of cultural focus is especially acute in the case of the companies that need it most.

Culture is a bit of an anomaly; culture in itself doesn't necessarily produce anything. Corporate culture often cannot be detected from afar. At times, the value of the culture can go unnoticed for long periods.

While an organization's culture can be silent, hard to see from afar, and perhaps misunderstood, culture is also a lightning rod for businesses. When a culture is strong, the business can overcome a lot of adversity. When a culture is weak, it will break under the pressure of just about anything - including opportunity.

It's hard to explain a great culture and within a weak culture, the elements are rarely recognized. Especially by those that are most affected by a weak, inner-collective mindset.

However, it isn't as hard to see culture if you look for it. There are many signs of a strong culture, as well as many signs for a weak culture. Here are some specific signs, and some questions, for leaders to ask when looking at your company culture.

KEY CHARACTERISTICS TO A STRONG CULTURE

Trust: In a high trust culture things can be done quickly. Change is made with less resistance, and feedback is delivered honestly and frequently. In your organization, do people politic and "dance around the issue" as to not offend or stir things up?

Engagement: The employees are focused on their roles and highly engaged on a daily basis. People know what is expected of them and they are comfortable asking questions if they ever get off track.

Commitment: When looking at commitment it comes down to attitude and aptitude. Does the team understand their mission? If so: are they behind it?

Celebration: Winning early and often creates strong culture. Celebrating those wins – both big and small – is common in strong cultures. Does your organization celebrate its successes?

Initiative: Often times going too far above and beyond can be problematic. However, when it comes to culture, strong ones have high-initiative employees. Initiative is rooted in the trust and commitment within the organization. Do your employees and co-workers take the ball - or pass it?

Loyalty: Great companies with great cultures tend to have extremely happy team members. They speak highly of their work, their leadership, their organization. What do you and your co-workers say about your company?

Productivity: In any organization, getting things done is key. The better the culture, the more things that are getting done. There's little micromanagement required in a strong and healthy organization. Does your company have high levels of "Get It Done?"

Communication: People need to communicate with reciprocity, not just memos and email. The root of every trait above starts here and ends with trust – and that's especially true for communication. How does your organization communicate?

KEY CHARACTERISTICS TO A WEAK CULTURE

In many cases the inverse of strong culture traits, these are some common signs in weaker cultures.

Blamestorming: Ever since I heard this phrase I have latched onto it. The habit of finding someone to blame resonates and infects weak cultures. Do people in your organization seek someone to blame? Do they learn from mistakes and move quickly to correct errors, without repeating them?

Turnover: An easy litmus test: If people are fleeing, then things are not good in "Your-org-town." While the occasional turnover happens and house cleaning is sometimes needed during times of change, turnover (as a whole) is not a good thing. Are people in your organization actively looking to leave or leaving?

Uncertainty: Another way to say "lack of confidence", uncertainty can be seen in many areas. Uncertainty can involve company direction, leadership capabilities, simple processes and procedures, and so on. Are your employees in the know with respect to what is important to them?

Fear: Right next to uncertainty lives fear. Sometimes these sentiments are actually created in each other's' shadows. Fear creates slow and unproductive employees who don't trust or communicate. Does your organization use fear to drive outcomes?

Blurred Vision: Vision becomes blurred for a number of reasons, but most often from a complete breakdown in communication throughout an organization. More times than not, the vision is there – but the people don't know it, or they don't hear it consistently. Does everyone in your company understand the vision?

While there are other more subtle signs and symptoms of health within a culture, the above represent some of the most apparent traits of disparate culture types.

Like most other critical components to corporate success, culture isn't something that can be changed overnight. However, if the goal is to improve the culture (and it should be no matter how strong your culture may be), then that objective must be worked on continuously. For leaders, you have to think about culture as a daily goal – much like sales, marketing, or finance.

With such intangible results and often unquantifiable outcomes, culture doesn't always get the attention it deserves. Culture has been one of the great vanishing acts within leadership conversations, business analysis, and executive education. I'm not sure why it has received the proverbial hall pass, but I suspect it's because culture is one of the harder things to measure and ultimately quantify.

A great vision, coupled with sound strategy, will fall flat on its face if the culture is weak. This inevitable fall happens because, in the end, success all comes down to people. The people are the ingredients that make the proverbial entree of company success. If the trust, communication, and "Get It Done" traits of a strong culture (among others) exist, good things will happen. And if they don't... your company will just be "Everybody Else."

WARNING:
EIGHT SIGNS OF
DYSFUNCTIONAL MANAGEMENT

Tweet This:

> *I believe most people are more intelligent than you may think. If your management is dysfunctional, you won't be able to hide it!*

Great businesses depend on people, ideas, communication, and vision to drive consistently desirable outcomes. Built on the back of hard work, clear objectives and determination, success can be within the reach of any organization. All of these traits must be guided by an executive leadership team – a team that knows how to get the best from the organization. But what about when that guidance and leadership doesn't happen?

What about when the management team doesn't drive performance? Or worse – they create dysfunction?

There may be no faster death of a great idea (or a great business) than a dysfunctional management team. But do you know the signs to watch for? If you catch them early, then perhaps you can do something to improve the situation. But, once struck by more than a few of these leadership killers, there may be no turning back.

Is your management team dysfunctional?

Here are eight signs to look for – as well as some thoughts on how to address the issue for business owners, managers, and employees.

- **Because I Said So:** If the only reason that you are given to complete a task is "because management said so", then you are in a bad situation. This behavior is an iteration of fear-based leadership, which is never going to drive high level performance. Often, this tactic can yield to employee paralysis, as team members become afraid to act due to potential repercussions.

- **Passive-Aggressive:** Whether it is showing up late to meetings, forgetting to share important details or consistent excuses for not getting things done, these behaviors are damaging in all cases. For instance, the late arrival to a meeting once can be an accident. Regularly showing up late is a sign of indifference, and can likely be a sign that the person doesn't care about the meeting's agenda, or attendees, or both. In strong cultures, this untimely behavior is nipped in the bud, but in a dysfunctional environment this passive-aggressive time management can be seen throughout the workplace.

- **Narcissistic:** When management (individual or as a team) is obsessed with their own individual success, it is a huge red flag. To lead, management must serve those on the front line. Upon driving performance, management will get their due recognition. However,

155

when the sole purpose is to feed the ego and support the growth of management, you can count on rampant dysfunction and less then desirable results.

- **Non-Committal:** Strategy of the week, the day or the hour? A terrible feeling for an employee is sensing that their direction is changing faster than the weather in Chicago. While change can be adapted more rapidly in a stronger culture, in a weak or dysfunctional culture, the fragile nature of the employees can be broken by even positive change.

- **Turn-Over:** Are you seeing a revolving door of people? People leaving your ranks is a really bad sign, and something that needs to be quickly rectified. If employees are leaving, whether by choice or not, then you can be fairly certain that management is dysfunctional. Hiring is never an exact science and the elimination of low performers is important. However, companies with high turn-over are often victims of weak culture and poor leadership. The rapid change of people is a Band-Aid, where management tries to cover up for a much bigger problem – a problem that they can find in the mirror.

- **Division:** When members of the management team intentionally or even unintentionally drive division between members of functional areas, you are staring dysfunction in the eye. Even though companies are generally divided into cross functions to cover the various areas of operations, synergy is still the great whole rather than the sum of its parts. Creating division within teams is often done with negative intent and may be used to cover up larger problems and to protect agendas. Protectionism never yields improved performance.

- **Politics:** Interoffice politics are a plague in business. I refer to this political sign as "exponentially dysfunctional management." A management team or individual driven by political gain (which can be a promotion, visibility or other). This individual gain, in a leader, may be the absolute worst. When it becomes obvious that management is acting on an agenda that isn't in the best interest of meeting the goals/mission of the enterprise as a whole, then you have a big problem.

- **(Mis)Communication or Lack thereof:** If the respective leaders of the organization do not know what is going on, you can be certain that the dysfunction has spread to the core of the operation. When the leadership team stops speaking and communicating to one another or they are trying to collect information from the rank and file it is time to worry. Strong leadership teams communicate early and often. They understand important messaging and they know what and when to share. When leadership teams become out of sync, due to dysfunction, you will see massive breakdowns in communication that start at the top – and radiate to the bones of the company.

ADDRESSING THE ISSUE

For business owners and employers: If you are seeing these behaviors throughout your organization, then you need to quickly grab a hold of the problem and address it head-on. These cultural problems will almost never rectify themselves. As I mentioned, bad leadership behaviors will tend to spread like disease – until they kill the business, either literally or metaphorically.

Every business deals with small cultural challenges from time to time. These changes can be brought on by a plethora of reasons. However, allowing cultural challenges to fester within the company is highly problematic.

While the biggest culprits of these transgressions are probably not reading this book – and certainly not doing anything about their organizational problems. Perhaps we, as leaders, can help. There are always those in high places that seek to be the agent of change. To change dysfunction you must seek it out, address it, and eliminate it.

Sometimes that means hard decisions, like eliminating managers who have perpetuated bad behavior, even if they were once very effective.

One guaranteed way not to improve the situation is to think it will take care of itself.

For employees: If you relate to these cautionary tales, that emotion should serve as a warning sign that your organization is in bad shape. Great companies rarely have great dysfunction, and great leaders rarely tolerate it. While changing positions is not always an option, I do highly recommend an attempt to address the problem with leadership (if possible), and always have a backup plan. Working within a dysfunctional environment is a surefire way to stunt your professional development, and limit your opportunities moving forward.

SHOULD MANAGERS BEFRIEND EMPLOYEES IN THE WORKPLACE?

Tweet This:

With our lives being drawn closer together by technology, can we draw a line in the sand between managers and employees?

IN THE BEGINNING

When I was growing up my father was always really tough on me, and I thought it was really unfair. I had several friends who had what I determined to be "cool" parents. What did I consider cool? The parental types that tried harder to be friends with their kids than they did to be parents to them.

When I would approach my dad about having a relationship more like that of my friends with "cool" parents, my father would often reply the same way.

"How am I supposed to be a good parent, who teaches you right from wrong, if I'm busy trying to be your friend?"

At the time I really didn't care about his answer. I didn't want to know wrong from right. I wanted to have a cool dad: one that my friends liked, one that didn't challenge me to do well in school, one that wouldn't tell me when I was acting like an imbecile.

I mean, why in the world would a child need to know right from wrong? All we really need is friends. The need for friends, and nothing more, is a scientifically proven fact… according to my non-scientific research of Facebook relationships.

I digress.

The role has reversed, and now I'm the parent. I am dealing with my own pair of children. They are great kids who, like all kids, need constant parenting. The best parenting I can offer is what I focus on giving them. Even though, at times, I want nothing more than to be their friend.

AS THE WORKPLACE TURNS

The workplace today isn't much different in terms of how we deal with the sensitive nature of relationships.

We have entered a world where our entire lives are out in the open and there isn't much that separates our work, family, community, etc.

This openness wasn't all brought about by choice. We have been forced into the open, with the proliferation of technology and social networking. But nonetheless the results are the same: we have been forced into the social stream, and become a part of the ever-present tech.

While there is no doubt that employees are not "children", there is a striking resemblance to the delicate relationship between an employer and their employee. Given that most of us spend half or our conscious life working, it isn't surprising that we want to have a bond greater than just colleagues with our co-workers. With so little time to enjoy social activities, sometimes our co-workers are the only social contact we have.

While that isn't necessarily ideal, the workplace environment does lead to friendships being born between employees.

As the employer, these relationships can be a bit of a quagmire.

When the professional relationship takes a social turn, that change can create complexities for providing the proper leadership and guidance. Can you be a leader, and be a friend? Or are these ideas mutually exclusive?

EMPLOYEE – EMPLOYEE RELATIONSHIPS

Friendship among the co-workers is certainly going to happen. Work is more enjoyable when we work with people we consider to be our friends. Friendly interoffice relationships are something that leadership shouldn't deter. However, there is one important thing that must be considered.

If employees have an overly satisfying social relationship, will they hold each other accountable for performance?

While it isn't necessarily the employees' responsibility to manage one another, they often do within the highest performing organizations.

I have found it unequivocally true that when one employee challenges their colleague to step up their game, that request has a more lasting effect than when management makes the same challenge. I think the response has to do with the purity that comes from one employee to another. That purity may not exist in the manager/employee relationship.

EMPLOYEE – EMPLOYER RELATIONSHIPS: ADDING COMPLEXITY

What about when a friendship is born between a Manager and Employee?

This relationship becomes more complicated.

It is VERY important that you recognize the risk associated with these types of relationships, so you can better manage them. While it may not be possible to entirely prevent friendships with subordinates, you have to consider the potential pitfalls.

The executive must make sure that the professional part of the relationship is solid, before allowing any level of social engagement. This type of friendship is no different than the relationship between employees but with higher stakes.

So often, a manager falls on their face because they believe that being the "cool" leader is going to yield better results. The logic is that being "cool" will keep them on the inside with the employees.

In some cases, a higher level of social engagement between the ranks may yield a higher state of awareness for activities within the company. However, there's no guarantee that visibility will increase.

What happens when the manager has to face a befriended employee on an issue of performance?

This confrontation is rarely considered when the relationship is being created. However, this necessary engagement can be the executive's worst nightmare, when performance has to be addressed.

The employer cannot allow their leadership to be trivialized by an unwillingness to face the performance issue head-on, no matter what the relationship looks like. Often the failure of leadership is that they don't address problematic performance early enough. Some executives believe that poor performance will rectify itself. When friendship exists, that ignored incompetence can jeopardize an entire organization.

SOLVING THE ISSUE?

There is one way that this friendship crisis can be mitigated, but it is by no means a perfect solution.

The employer MUST properly set the expectations up front for performance. Whether a small organization, or a large one, guidelines create a clear path for communication between parties. Clear rules and expectations are a basis for any difficult conversations that may occur. While clear guidelines are crucial for every manager and every employee, these guidelines become crucial if that leadership relationship becomes social.

By no means can a perfect science, clearly articulated expectations and regular discussions around outcomes minimize the hard feelings that come when someone you like becomes someone that isn't getting it done.

You know, sometimes when my dad took me out back and played catch with me it was kind of like playing with a friend. We were doing something we liked together and there was no problem with that.

But when we went back inside the house it was still expected that I kept my room tidy, the lawn mowed, and my grades above par. If I didn't, there were repercussions!

I knew what was expected of me, but deep down he was still a big cool guy that was teaching me about life. In other words, he was cooler than I was willing to admit. And he still is.

The workplace doesn't have to be out-of-bounds for friendships, even among executives and employees. You can like those you lead and lead those you like. But you must understand the nuance that comes with these relationships, and plan and act accordingly.

WE DON'T NEED NO STINKIN' NEGATIVITY

Tweet This:

A little reality is fine, but being negative just to be negative has no place online or in the office.

In the world we live in, we can get all of the bad news we could ever hope for in one click. Furthermore, we only have a limited amount of time to accomplish what we need to get done - and that leaves only so much time to spend on Social Media. This limited time can become further convoluted between Twitter, Facebook, LinkedIn, Google+, Klout, Empire Avenue, and a plethora of other options to devote our time and resources. To be successful we MUST commit our time and our attention to our goals.

One of these goals should be to avoid the rash of negativity that exists in social spaces. There are people in social channels that are strictly there to "stir the pot". They aren't there to add to the conversation, bring new ideas, or even thoughtful criticism (I'm good with healthy debate – I am not suggesting that people shouldn't engage in offering different viewpoints). Nope, I'm talking about the folks who are strictly there to ruin your online experience, and the experience of others.

To this I say…

Ban, Block, Ignore, Reject, don't waste even a second paying attention to these people. In a space with hundreds if not thousands of people in which you can create a meaningful connection, why in the world would you waste your time on negativity?

As an example, I recently had a good friend who has been working on an amazing cause in the social media space. His cause has the potential to change people in a powerful way, and provides a positive message that creates good will - if even for just a moment. Many people have rallied around this message; they have found it a valuable and easily-shared cause that will make a difference.

However, like so many others who bring a positive light to the social stream, there are the naysayers. These naysayers are the ones who feel obligated to poke holes in the cause, in a way that seems nothing more than self-serving. (I opt not to name names as I don't see it accomplishing anything meaningful).

Bottom line, interactions are your experience. Just like "out there" in the world, you get to choose who you do and don't want to engage.

My Recommendation: Choose wisely and leave the bullies and headcases to divide and conquer one another, on their own time, without your participation. After all, if we don't respond to them, they will have to respond to each other.

THE PEOPLE-CENTERED ORGANIZATION

Tweet This:

It doesn't matter how good your processes are if you don't recognize that your people are the key to success.

At one point or another, every business was a startup. Berkshire Hathaway, Goldman Sachs, Microsoft, and on and on. While few startups will ever become Fortune 500 companies, many organizations grow up and become fluid ecosystems that live and grow, both in revenue and in human resource. Gaining maturity, organizations arrive at a point where the growing demand on its resources requires the implementation of processes and procedures in order to facilitate continued growth.

For the most part, acquiring new resources is a part of the business life cycle. As a company matures, its day-to-day needs become more complex, its systems require more maintenance and support, and its customers demand higher levels of attention.

Growing pains are all enviable issues born of a good idea being brought to life; usually by an entrepreneur who brings passion, and perhaps their livelihood, in exchange for the opportunity to realize their dream.

In its infancy, business is all about aching toward growth. As the business blossoms, the company must add the required human resources to meet the growing demand. With each new person comes a new cog in the wheel.

Often, early in a business' life, the people bring an entrepreneurial sensibility to the entrepreneurial organization. Much like the owner, they bring a high level of enthusiasm with them each and every day. However, as the business continues to grow, each new hire becomes further removed from the founders. With this distance comes risk – a risk of not embedding into the tightly-knit culture that the company once had.

Many times newfound growth leads a business to become more rigid, rendering its day-to-day operations to be defined by the "Three P's" (Process, Procedure, and Politics). The best people no longer find growth; the best are supplanted by those most willing to participate in the new game – a game that's based on the Three P's. Sadly, this hiring phenomenon perpetuates in organization after organization as they aim to follow the textbook for how to grow businesses through rigid processes and political hierarchy.

For the past few years, I have taught MBA Level Strategy in the Chicago suburbs. The course I teach is a second-year MBA course, and tends to be one of the final courses taken by MBA students before they finish their degree.

Every year, I find myself straying farther and farther from the material in the textbook. I gravitate more and more toward a new strategic concept: *"The People Centered Organization."*

The philosophy is not new at all but it has been relegated to a 'back burner' status, as companies focus more tightly on wealth, greed, and power; aiming to gain strength by replacing human capital with the Three P's.

The conundrum of people vs. the Three P's lies in that the tradeoff is non-progressive. Not because processes don't enhance profitability; I would be the first to raise my hand and say that they do, can, and should. However, the operative word is "Enhance." With better processes, companies have opportunity to optimize execution ergo achieve greater margin. Process, Profit, and Profitability don't move an organization forward if people aren't at the center of the conversation.

Ponder this. When these streamlined processes (engineered by "World Class Business Minds") are implemented, how are they managed? Who does the work that is left? Who is benchmarking the newfound success? Who will continue the required evolution (and revolution) of the process?

Who will ensure that over time the most recent best practice implemented won't become obsolete? Which makes your new practice, in essence, the next outdated one. Your business is becoming a mere lifecycle of changing best practices - practices that ALWAYS need to be implemented by people.

The answer is simply profound ... People. In business, the "P" that truly matters is People.

The center of any organizational ecosystem is people. Not processes, not information systems, not killer products or technology. Simply, profoundly, flesh, blood, heart, and soul. This concept is proven time and again by companies with very simple models and 'me too' products realizing great success. Think Southwest Airlines, Google, or Under Armour. Southwest wasn't the first commercial airlines, Google didn't invent search, and Under Armour surely didn't invent sports apparel. These companies saw market opportunities and they pounced on them with stellar execution by stellar people. Once again, these companies proved that great people can take common ideas to uncommon results.

The moment when organizations forget that people provide their heart beat, their life blood, is the exact same moment that company is putting itself on life support.

Growing entities need structure; there is no denying this basic tenet. However, any business that trades its people for process is bound to be a poor business. Those that do survive will do so riddled with weak culture and troubled morale.

In my classroom, where we discuss strategy development and execution, I have a theme. Every student who leaves my class will know and remember this theme as they set out to start and drive tomorrow's great organizations...

"When, and only when, a company recognizes that its people are its most valued asset will that business truly have the opportunity for greatness."

WHEN A NEW HIRE DOESN'T WORK OUT

Tweet This:

Hiring is an imperfect science. Once you recognize you've made a mistake, don't make another one.

It's an exciting time within any organization when we grow. As entrepreneurs and leaders we aspire to increase our teams and add talent within our workplace. In fact, we often speculate that the very core of the entrepreneur's role is to be a "Job Creator."

For any leader, HR professional, or other hiring manager, you are familiar with the trials and tribulations of recruitment. Finding great talent that fits into your culture is no easy task.

With all of the predictive tests, pre-employment verification, reference checks, and (of course) your self-proclaimed expert people skills, you would expect that we would make a great hire every time. Never (rarely) do we make a hire and say to ourselves, "Gee, I'm not so sure."

Of course we're sure, if we were not sure then why in the world would we make the hire in the first place?

174

Many times the success of an organization, especially a smaller business, comes down to making more strong hires than weak ones. Strong and weak, similar to good and bad, are subjective terms. But anyone that has done substantial hiring has their way of describing the challenge in finding a good hire, not a bad one... The goal in most organizations is to get it right more than we get it wrong.

So what happens if we don't get it right? It isn't so much a question of if, but when, a hiring mistake will happen. The causes can be many. Even in the most stringent hiring processes, the chosen candidate just doesn't work out.

In small business, for instance, we often make the mistake of hiring "Too Close to Home." This is the phenomenon of hiring a friend, former colleague, or neighbor because we believe it is easier than going through a full recruitment process. Often times, following this method allows for a strong foundation that takes mystery out of the equation. The idea of hiring among friends can just as easily backfire. When a friendly hire doesn't work out, it creates an incredibly awkward situation.

In larger organizations there are also a plethora of events that lead to a bad hire, including the wrong recruiting platform, the wrong interview questions, or the lack of time to go through the abundance of resumes.

Nevertheless, no business is exempt; bad hires happen, so what can you do about it?

This may come across as a bit brazen, but I'm going to make the conclusion here simple. When you as a leader begin to sense that the hiring decision was a bad one, quick action is the only remedy. And by acting quickly I mean an immediate notice for the person to right the ship – or, more likely, a notice of termination.

I offer this with substantial empathy in mind as someone that has allowed bad hires to linger for too long, costing both time and money. Sadly, the lingering has never led to a great change in result or in a change of my initial gut feelings.

One thing that most leaders have is a gut intuition. You have that sense for when something is going well and when something doesn't. What many of us also have is substantial empathy which can lead us to hanging on too long. While empathy is acceptable, underperforming behavior is not. We lead, therefore we must act.

So I leave you with the following conclusions:

- When it doesn't work out you must remedy it quickly... (Action to right the ship)

- By remedy I mean change the situation... (Reassign, Terminate)

- As leaders we must recognize that our empathy to a few (The bad decision, Hire) can become a burden to the many (Everyone else that is carrying the weight)...

- When your gut speaks... listen (Learn from your past experience)

MINIMIZING TRANSITION DURING TRANSFORMATION

Tweet This:

People by nature are change averse. But you have to keep them focused during change because it is constant.

Due to the high pace of proliferation surrounding us, information and technology have become rapidly more available to everyone.

What used to be considered "radical transformation" is now merely "change", within many organizations.

With each iteration of innovation comes more knowledge. That knowledge, being the byproduct of information and context, makes us more and more aware of the change around us. For most people that awareness is scary.

It wasn't long ago that businesses ran with modest, almost unnoticeable change year after year. Employment was a lifelong commitment for employers and employees alike.

For the human psyche, this commitment was ideal. Deep down, people don't like change. It isn't so much because change is a bad thing. Most people, in fact, would probably suggest that change is a good thing.

However, the same group of people who embrace change as a concept will become scared, resistive, or even combative when that change directly affects them.

When the change was unexpected and/or unprepared for, it tends to yield less than satisfactory results. Your opinion on change doesn't really matter at that point; human nature takes over.

So if change creates problems, what happens within an organization when transformation rears its beautiful yet unforgiving head?

During typical organizational transformation employees can quickly become lost. Sometimes a lack of direction is due to their own fear of what they see on the horizon. With fear of change looming in their minds, some employees will stand on the precipice of mass exodus. As a leader, you stand to lose key employees that were outside of the "Transformation Planning."

When this shift happens, turnover can be cancerous within a delicate culture. Beyond cultural disruption, turnover is extraordinarily expensive – and it also slows down the transformative goals, which is how we arrived here in the first place.

To add insult to injury, some organizations choose to blame the exiting employees. While this blamestorming is easy (kind of like sales saying "Price" cost them the deal) it is nothing more than a scape goat; simply suggesting that some employees weren't "moving with the times" shows both a lack of character and a lack of class.

Further, a blamestorming statement like that one is most likely not true.

This brings us to the first point of action…

As an organizational leader, you must constantly evaluate employee fit into the culture and their ability to adapt to change. Then you must do everything in your power to motivate those to align their efforts to the company direction.

Then you must re-center your thinking, and focus on what you can control.

After all, as leaders you are ALWAYS responsible for setting the sails of the proverbial ships. We all know that a ship will move faster and more on course with all hands on deck. Just look for that "Motivation" poster in your office… you know, the one that says "Teamwork."

Bringing the ownership of transformation to YOU, the leaders of change.

While we cannot control the entire domino effect that coincides with an organization's shift, we most certainly have control of most of it.

These important elements of change include the messaging between leadership and the team, as well as the creation and cultivation of a culture of change.

The transformational organization isn't going away. In fact, change and transformation are going to see an exponential increase in speed.

Just look at what is happening around us for the cues.

While we cannot reverse the trend of rapid change, we can control our outcomes. Influencing your outcomes starts with great people, and ends with great leaders.

Shift happens… how will you make the most of it?

CHARACTER AND BACK-STABBING

Tweet This:

People by nature are change averse. But you have to keep them focused during change because it is constant.

Of all the quotes I have read and seen there may not be one out there that resonates with me more than the following quote by Eleanor Roosevelt:

"Great minds discuss ideas; average minds discuss events; small minds discuss people."

What do you say about others when they aren't around?

Every day we are fortunate enough to have (ideally) many interactions with others. The opportunity to exchange words and ideas with friends, family, colleagues and even strangers is important. In these interactions, we find the hope of gaining knowledge, wisdom, and experience that we can somehow apply to positively influence those in our lives.

While engaging in these vast and varied dialogues, I find that "people" do become part of, if not the center of, discussion. And while Roosevelt's quote is profound, it isn't always realistic to spend your time "ideating." In a world where we are constantly affected by the decisions of other individuals, people will be discussed. The question becomes: how do you discuss people in a way that's productive?

All too often a conversation leads to a "behind the back" diatribe on the inadequacy of others. Perhaps that diatribe is truly warranted, based on the person's actions. For the sake of your character, I suggest that you steer away from contributing to such conversations. As a leader, you should perhaps show the courage to challenge such exchanges, as they are rarely productive or meaningful in the bigger picture. Here are four reasons to rise above these negative exchanges…

- **Transparency:** If you engage in these types of people-exchanges, it shows a lot about the person you are. The willingness to sit around and negatively discuss others reveals that you may not have much to add, especially if you are shooting down others' thoughts and ideas.

- **Reciprocity:** If you are giving me an earful about someone else, then I can pretty much assume that you will do the same to me when I'm not around. Even if this is untrue, I'm going to struggle to believe otherwise. Wouldn't you?

- **Maturity:** High School is over. It's time to grow up a bit. If you have an issue with someone that is worth fixing, then confront the person directly. As people always say, don't say anything behind someone's back that you won't say to their face. (Heed this advice; it is a good litmus test for future conversations).

- **Character:** Overall, talking about someone negatively behind his or her back shows a lack of character. All the positive public commentary in the world cannot overcome the effect of negative chatter.

The art of steering away from negatively discussing others is not an easy one. I feel safe in saying that we all engage in this kind of dialogue from time to time. Sometimes frustration, disdain, or peer pressure can make it easy to fall into this trap.

What I am recommending is to be cognizant of the behavior. Aspire to limit and remove this activity from your life. Focus on worthwhile and constructive negative conversations directly, especially if you have negative feelings about someone. If the issue isn't worth a direct conversation, then the subject certainly isn't worth your time.

Take my Mom's advice (whether she lived it or not), "If you don't have something good to say about someone, then don't say it at all," and then add to the quote "…unless it is to their face"

Your character is critical to your success. Don't trivialize your role as a leader by acting like a teenager. A sign of maturity is a willingness to confront worthwhile problems. Make sure you spend your time talking about bigger things.

Be the one… to rise above!

SOCIAL RECRUITING:
I'M A BELIEVER

Tweet This:

No matter how others decide to behave, you have the choice to rise above.

SETTING THE STAGE FOR GROWTH

Recently our organization decided to hire a new national channels team, to aid in meeting our key strategic initiatives for the year. We knew we had a big task ahead of us. The new team would consist of four high-caliber individuals, with a background in collaboration technology, and we wanted to have the team in place within 90 days.

As a smaller organization, we don't have a large HR department to handle screening, first interviews, background checks, etc. In our case, we are part of the process – so, when we are busy working on hiring, it can often be a distraction from what needs to be done day in and day out.

Knowing that we were making a substantial investment into the future, we knew what we needed. First and foremost we needed to make great hires as turnover here wouldn't work.

We needed a plan to find and sift through great talent quickly, so we could get to interviewing – and more importantly, to quickly on-boarding the new team members.

A LOT OF OPTIONS, NOT MANY GOOD ONES

Thankfully, we have moved beyond the help wanted ads in the local paper (for the most part, I believe there still is a help wanted section – is that true?) The internet has certainly made simple help wanted advertising possible. However, for all of the technology out there, a lot of the recruitment methods haven't advanced that quickly.

So when the decision was made to make these hires, we had to review our recruiting options.

- **Traditional Job Boards** *(Monster, CareerBuilder, and Trade Association)*: For the past several years these websites have been the recruiting tools for small business and corporate HR alike. The problem with these sites is they attract far more irrelevant and unqualified applicants than highly qualified, targeted candidates. So with little time to waste, this option was eliminated.

- **Headhunters:** For some very specific positions I can see the value of headhunters. However, with the information available nowadays on the interwebs, I see less and less need for paid recruiting. For us, there was no way I was going to pay 10% or more of the budget for the new hires to a headhunter. I would rather have those dollars for negotiation with the best possible candidates. Therefore, headhunters also didn't make the final cut.

- **Social Recruiting** *(LinkedIn, Facebook)*: With 100 million+ users on LinkedIn, and nearly 10x that on Facebook (as I write this), there is a great opportunity to use Social Tools to recruit. Consider: Connections of connections with great skills – as well as a Job Posting capability via both platforms – well, this had to be the medium. We decided to post a very specific position description for two positions on LinkedIn, and away we went.

THE RESULTS

After two 30-day ads, we finalized our team. In my opinion we were able to obtain talent that far exceeded even what we had originally anticipated. We additionally posted the jobs to our update statuses on LinkedIn and Facebook, as well as several specific groups.

The LinkedIn advertisements and other social posts yielded more than 400 applicants, of which 300+ were qualified. Those numbers made the resume reviews tricky, but gave us no shortage of great candidates.

While the success of the hires is to be determined, I can't begin to tell you what a relief it was to see the success of these platforms for our recruitment needs.

DEGREES OF SEPARATION

We are all familiar with the degrees of separation that are created via Social Networks. As it turns out, of the four hires we made, three of them were known entities to at least one member of our current team.

While I'm not surprised, I was simply amazed: we really do seemingly know everyone.

Using the Social Recruitment method, we were able to hire highly qualified candidates from a tremendous field of applicants. We even ended up with the benefit of hiring relatively known entities, and that often limits the risk of a hiring mistake.

AN OBSERVATION AND A PREDICTION

I don't think I'm making any great prediction here when I say that CareerBuilder, Monster, and other traditional job boards are in big trouble. Between their minimal Social presence and the sprawling reach of Social Networks to bring together candidates and companies, I simply cannot find a need for these types of sites.

I feel comfortable saying these sites will end up a skeleton of what they once were. They may very well end up as parked URLs sooner rather than later.

THE NEXT HIRE(S)

Few things in my world warrant a solid recommendation (Reputation is key!).

Social Recruitment, however, is one that does. I cannot say enough about the potential ROI that can be attained through a well-planned Social Search for your next team member.

While Social Searching may not be a new concept to many people, I still hear horror story after horror story about finding and hiring great talent. For those that have experienced this horror, it is time to get Social with your recruiting efforts.

While I have flirted with Social Searching in the past, I can now say after doing it that I'm definitely a believer!

GLOBAL TECHNOLOGY STEPPING UP COLLABORATION

Tweet This:

I don't know if there is anything more impactful in our businesses than how we interact with technology.

For anyone that can remember the time when the latest and greatest technology emerged to bring business to the next level, the impact that these advancements actually make on companies is profoundly interesting.

Some can probably remember the days before email and before cell phones, when letters were typed by hand and traveling sales people had to actually stop at a pay phone to verify an appointment, or call home to check in.

More than ever, management needs to be watching technology trends and making sure their organization is equipped.

Times are changing, the proliferation of technology is moving faster than ever, and businesses are the ones that are benefiting. At least they should be!

There are many ways that technology is leading to better business practices. There are systems for managing customers, accounting, communications, and operations. We are connected 24×7 (if we so choose) and we are able to reach all ends of the world instantly via the click of a button.

As a proponent of successful businesses being comprised of people that use technology and not just technology alone, I believe that nothing in business may be more affected by emerging technology than Human Resources. Recruiting, talent development, and employee retention are all seeing a significant boost based upon what advances in technology have to offer.

Two of the specific technologies that are revolutionizing talent and professional development more than any are IP (Internet Protocol) Based Communications such as Skype, VoIP, and Video Conferencing as well as the rapid emergence of Social Media (LinkedIn, Twitter, Facebook, Google+).

Let's take a look across the scope of Talent Management and explore how the aforementioned technologies as well as a few others are facilitating success for so many companies.

RECRUITING NEW TALENT

"Help Wanted": It used to be a newspaper ad or a sign in the window. Your audience was narrow and your options were thin. It was difficult to reach the best talent, leaving positions to be filled by less than ideal candidates.

- **Communications** – With the ability to inexpensively bring employees in via the network either by voice, video, or perhaps a combination such as WebEx, employees can now be sourced from and potentially located anywhere. Productivity tools allow companies to hire the BEST candidate from any location and get her integrated with the team, whether near or far.

- **Social Media** – Depending on the specifics of the job, talent can be sought through massive global social networks such as Linked In, Facebook, and Twitter, as previously discussed. These networks allow a help wanted ad to reach millions of users who may or may not be actively seeking employment. Recruiting and searching for talent has also never been easier due to profiles, recommendations, and other affiliations that can be easily found online using Social Media. As an aside, Social Media has also helped many companies decide who not to hire.

TALENT DEVELOPMENT

Training used to be a quarterly or yearly trip to headquarters (for remote employees) and classroom learning for those already in town. Coordinating training was intensive and time consuming. With technology advances, learning can now be routine, meaningful, and completed on demand.

- **Communications** – Similar to the recruiting process, the continued education of employees can be accomplished using technology tools. Webinars, Distance Learning, and E-Learning platforms all pave the way for continued education for employees regardless of where they are located. On top of being able to create content and have employees learn and develop on demand, it also helps companies to utilize global resources to provide the education.

- **Social Media** – Intranets have existed for companies for some time, however they were rarely used all that effectively. With professional usage of social platforms, employees can learn from one another as well as competitors by following, reading, and embracing the information that is widely available. Content is created and shared regularly, and that sharing allows company talent to keep their finger on the pulse of the industry and any important internal company changes.

EMPLOYEE RETENTION

Turnover has a huge impact on a business, as I've mentioned before. Whether near or far from headquarters, companies need to focus on how they can keep people satisfied, growing, and engaged. In the past, when companies would hire remote employees, they oft felt isolated and/or disconnected from the organization. With emails and phone calls being the only regular communication, eventually the disconnected employee may choose to be with an organization where they feel more involved. Technology has changed that disconnection. If used correctly, technology can assist the organization with retention, allowing the company to focus on strategy with key employees… rather than on replacing them.

1. **Communications** – Hearing a voice on the line is fine, it is practical, but like long distance relationships in life, eye contact means a lot. With offerings from Free (Skype), to immersive telepresence costing millions (Cisco, Polycom), and everything in between, companies and their employees can now sit across the table and make eye contact with the click of a mouse. As easy as a phone call, video can be accomplished – and the quality is really good. Video is not only beneficial for the employee, but also for the company. Video and eye contact forces focus and regular collaboration (we all know how easy it can be to multi-task on the phone). Another item that is critical to many employees is flexibility. With tools that allow productivity anywhere and everywhere, (pending signal), companies can be more flexible with their resources – allowing all parties to benefit

2. **Social Media** – Social is a medium for even smaller companies to build their brand, and create an identity for their employees. This social branding effort can often aid in the development of company community and - in some cases -successful friendships, outside of work. While peoples' activities outside of work generally don't bear much on the organization's success, happy people tend to generate more productivity. People that feel connected to their brand and that feel they are a part of something special tend to work harder and drive greater results. Social Media is a growing vehicle for accomplishing greater productivity in this regard.

For as long as business has been business, companies have only been as good as their people. In almost all cases where a great product or service fails, it isn't the product or service at all. Rather success or failure is all about the people behind it. With emerging communication technology and proper social media integration, you have the chance to be ahead of the curve.

Now technology of course isn't free, and choosing the technologies that are best for your organization may take some work. However, working on finding the right technology is time well spent. You can all but assume that the competition is looking at all the options, too. Some are integrating, some are watching and waiting and you can only hope that a few are oblivious. Nevertheless, technology will continue to advance – making companies faster, smarter, and full of better talent.

The question is, are you embracing technology, or are you hoping to ride to prosperity on the tired old horse that got you to where you are today?

DO YOUR MEETINGS HAVE MEANING?

Tweet This:

> *It's entirely too easy to become entrenched in meeting after meeting that accomplish nothing.* THE ILLUSION

> *"Well it has been a pleasure, Mr. Customer. I look forward to talking again soon."*

You shake hands, clasp your briefcase, and you proceed to exit the office.

As you approach the elevator, you adjust your tie (blouse, makeup, etc.) and step on with a bit of swagger, thinking to yourself: what a great meeting!

We laughed, we cried, we shared great stories. This is going to be a great long-term relationship.

And then, Houdini, it hits you…

THE REVELATION

Alright, so maybe the laugh was more of a friendly smile, and yeah, I know… those tears are more of a metaphor than anything.

Goodness, you think to yourself. I just spent an hour with that customer, and I have no idea what just happened. Surely there was an exchange and some important things were discussed. But there are no takeaways, no action items, no scheduled next meeting.

In the meantime the customer has already forgotten your name and your business card. Your pamphlets have already found their way into the circular file.

Then you ask yourself, "What the heck just happened?"

What happened was you just lost an hour, wasted a prospect's time and essentially had the type of meeting that has given meetings a bad name.

THE PROBLEM

Every day, across businesses of every type, meetings are conducted. Every hour, on the hour, we take a seat at the table.

We sit down with a purpose, or at least what we think is a purpose, in offices, boardrooms, restaurants and coffee shops.

We attempt to drive small talk to build rapport, and then perhaps we lead with questions to learn about the prospect's business.

Sometimes we don't ask questions at all, we just get in front of the customer and spew everything we know about our product and service – hoping that the customer is a slot machine and when we hit on the right feature their eyes will line up like cherries.

In some cases, we are meeting with people we know. Maybe these people are on our team, maybe they are long-time customers. Those meetings can be met with the same challenges. The comfort level can sometimes drive an even less-valuable exchange.

But in the end, whether with prospects, employees, or long term accounts, the problem is, our purpose isn't clear in our mind. Therefore you can be sure it isn't clear in theirs.

Curing Useless Meeting Disorder

Okay, so there is no such disorder. I made it up. However, I truly believe that there should be such a thing, because I know that it's real. I suspect you do, too.

In order to move business forward, we must communicate. Meetings, regardless of the medium, are important in this process.

To make meetings effective, a few specific things must happen.

Here are four elements I attempt to bring to every meeting. These four elements are designed to give meaning to every meeting.

- **Set the Agenda** – Big meetings like conferences and board meetings always have an agenda, but rarely is an agenda present for one-on-one meetings or small group settings. I even see team meetings where there is no agenda. Setting the agenda gives the opportunity to properly manage expectations up front. To make the meeting more useful, advance notice of the agenda is great so the other party can review, provide feedback, and be prepared for a valuable exchange.

- **Stick to the Plan (But be Flexible)** – Does that even make sense? It should. The point is: make sure that you stay on the agenda as much as possible. However, listen carefully for opportunity to explore important topics. Often times the information you are looking for is offered up if you listen carefully.

- **Value the Schedule** – I like to do this upfront. "Mr. Customer, we are on from 3:00pm – 4:00pm. Does that still work for you?" That confirmation courtesy shows anyone and everyone that you value their time - and yours. Time is money. Don't waste it.

- **Have Specific Action Items** – This piece one may be the most important element and the one most frequently missed. How often do you leave a meeting with no "specific" takeaway(s)? If you can look in the mirror and say rarely or never, then you are the "Meeting Master". Having said that, I have caught myself a few times becoming such a Master, and I'm not proud of it. So be specific: set the next engagement or action item. Put a time around it. Then do whatever it is you committed to. This commitment is how things get done.

Simple enough, or so it seems. But I challenge you to make every meeting productive with these four elements. Your customers and employees will thank you, and the results will speak for themselves.

12 WAYS TO SELL MORE Y-O-U

Tweet This:

People do buy based on relationships. So don't forget about the first sale.

We all want to sell more. Whether it is our job, or our lives, we are always selling.

Selling is a requisite to building meaningful business, customers, and friendships. Yet, sometimes we get so into selling our products and services that we forget where it all began.

Recently, while attending a conference, I had the opportunity to listen to David Nour speak. David wrote a book entitled *Relationship Economics*. While much of the content has been covered in one way or another before, he said one thing that I thought was quite profound.

"Everywhere but in the USA, people build relationships prior to getting involved in a business relationship; only here do we enter into business first and if and only if the transaction goes well do we build a relationship."

The statement got me to thinking about the act of building relationships, and the reminder that people buy from people they like.

Perhaps basics like these can help us turn things around for ourselves, our businesses, and even our economies.

So we start by selling ourselves, and let the rest happen on by itself. Here (in no particular order) are the 12 Most Necessary Actions to Sell More "You"

1. **Appearance:** Do you look the part? This isn't a suggestion that you have to be good looking, but rather a suggestion that when you are out "shaking hands and kissing babies" that you appear put-together and confident. And, in case you are wondering, a smile goes a long way.

2. **Empathetic:** Do you know what most peoples' favorite subject is? If not, here is a hint, it isn't you! Nope, it is themselves. People love to talk about themselves. When you take a genuine interest in others, it is much more likely they will like you.

3. **Knowledgeable:** Are you well aware of what is going on in the world? People want to be around people who they think are intelligently engaged with current events and other important issues. I'm not saying to delve into deep topics like politics and religion; I'm just saying it is good if you know what is going on with the "Big Picture" – before you start to dive into the details.

4. **Humor:** We aren't all comedians. Many of us aren't all that funny at all (this guy included). However, having a sense of humor is a good idea if you want to sell more you. Unless your goal is to be liked by primarily smug and miserable people, a bit of laughter goes a long way in relationship-building.

5. **Interesting:** Are you interesting? Do you have stories to tell, ideas to share, or…? When you are engaging with folks, they tend to gravitate towards people that are interesting. Note: This is not an invitation to be boastful, overly provocative, or just plain over the top. It is merely a suggestion to think about "adding" to the conversation.

6. **Humble:** Under "Interesting" I mentioned not be boastful. I will further that by saying: avoid bragging at all costs. Nobody genuinely likes a cocky person. Arrogance generally shows an insecurity, and frankly people aren't that interested in your "awesomeness". Try giving credit as often as possible, and do it genuinely. Then sit back and watch how much you that helps you sell!

7. **Honest:** If you don't have this one, you won't sell much Y-O-U at all. Perhaps you can manipulate here and there and even get ahead momentarily. However, violating trust is incredibly risky and is the absolute fastest way to the bottom of the ladder, in life and business. Be honest, make it count, then proceed to win trust.

8. **Diligent:** What type of follow through do you have? Do you always get it done, whatever "it" is? People really

like others that they can count on. Simple enough, moving on...

9. **Authentic:** I was reticent to put this one on the list. Authenticity is overused and in some spots it has lost meaning. However, there is a reason authenticity is so widely discussed. People like to be around people that they perceive as "real." While being real isn't exactly the same thing as honesty, this is a highly valuable trait. If you are seen as anything other than the genuine article, don't be surprised if you struggle to connect and sell more Y-O-U.

10. **Integrity:** Are you careful to always live the words you speak? Do you have a reputation of owning your mistakes and working hard to learn from them? People of high integrity have a gravity of their own that pulls people toward them. It isn't by accident that this magnetism happens, but it won't happen easily because integrity is a nonstop task.

11. **Adaptable:** People that can be genuine and honest all while being able to quickly adjust to unique situations around unique people, tend to do very well. Those that can stand out in many situations tend to sell a whole bunch of "Y-O-U."

12. **Presence:** The best definition I've ever heard of this: It is hard to put into words what this "Presence" is, but you know it when you see it, and when you do, you just can't help but be influenced by this person. Simple enough, do you have presence? While it may not be possible to have

all of these traits, the more you can illustrate in the presence of others the more "Y-O-U" that you will sell.

Don't believe me? Add these 12 to your repertoire and then let's chat. I'm certain if you execute, YOU will feel all the love and success that you could ever hope for.

HANDLING CRITICISM

Tweet This:

It is nice to get positive feedback. Now provide me some criticism so I can keep improving myself.

I've never met a person that couldn't take a compliment.

Of course I have met the vast landscape of personalities when dealing with positive feedback, but nevertheless they all tend to deal with the positive reinforcement quite well.

Some of the personalities are as follows:

- The extraordinarily humble: "Aww you shouldn't have"

- The "Pretend" humble: "Aww you shouldn't have, but since you did…"

- The balanced personality: "Why thank you very much, I appreciate the kind words"

- The slightly arrogant: "I did do a great job didn't I?"

And last but not least…

- The Egomaniac: "I am just that awesome, you are lucky that you are here talking to me right now."

All different reactions, yet the common bond is that all of these personalities enjoy receiving compliments.

ENTER CRITICISM

I've never met a person that genuinely appreciated criticism. Personally, both I and my fragile ego have issues with being critiqued.

In my life and travels, I have met the people who say they are okay with critical feedback (they cry at night) as well as the people who cannot handle it whatsoever (they cry at night... and during the day as well).

Criticism is rooted in many things. Difficult feedback can come from failure(s). However, a critical remark can also come from jealousy, insecurity, genuine empathy, hubris, as well as numerous other sources.

What is important to understand is that in the peaks and valleys of life, you will be criticized. In fact, the more successful you become the more likely you will be criticized. I liken it to the "Crabs in a Bucket" mentality; no matter what most people tell you, they don't want your success to be greater than their own.

With the connection between success and criticism in mind, you will have to learn to deal with both effectively. If you handle criticism well, your likelihood of success increases. If you allow disapproving comments to consume you, your reaction will impact your performance and your character.

Unfavorable reviews may never grow on you, but here are four things to apply to better deal with criticism.

1. **Be Humble:** When criticized, your rebuttal needs to be founded in strong character. Being angry and/or arrogant will not reflect well on you.

2. **Be Accepting:** Everyone is entitled to their opinion. Whether good, bad, right, wrong, every person has one. You don't have to accept that their disapproval is founded in fact or accuracy. But you do have to respect people are entitled to their opinions.

3. **Be Strong:** In dealing with criticism you must show strength. When a negative judgment is based in truth, it is important you focus on learning from your failure. When the criticism is based on opinion - or even worse, on lies - you must show strong character. Do not stoop to the lower level of those engaging in the negative dialogue.

4. **Be The Bigger Person:** State your case rationally, based on 1-3 above. Do not engage in a battle of who can scream the loudest. Remember, you can win the argument and still lose big in the process. Further, pick your battles. Not every act of criticism against you requires a response. Sometimes not responding is the best response.

At the core, criticism is simply the opinion of another. Whether you like it or not, your critics will come at you from now until kingdom come. Best to be prepared and to handle the inevitable like a pro.

How will you rise above?

THE FINE LINE BETWEEN EMPOWERMENT AND ISOLATION

Tweet This:

It is critical that we give our employees enough rope to accomplish great things. However, be sure the rope is noose free.

I think the buzzword phenomenon has finally backfired. Perhaps saying "finally" backfired is letting it off the hook too easily.

The latest trends in leadership actually fail all the time, but not necessarily because they are wrong. These ideas fail because the managers who read these "Next Big Thing" articles on HBR, *Forbes* or *Inc.* don't fully understand the concepts ...but decide to implement them anyway.

In a world that is served up regularly with "The Next Big Thing," I have recently seen an uptick in the calling for empowering employees; the (not so) new rage in today's world of "servant leadership" gurus.

I'm a fan of servant leadership. The desire to allow your employees the freedom to make decisions and become a part of the process is admirable AND worthwhile.

In theory, the empowered employee is created in an environment where leadership provides a clear organizational road map and couples this vision with guidelines to the company's expectations. The highly competent employee can feel greater flexibility to contribute more and ask for permission less. Ultimately, this empowerment allows them to do more of what they are capable of doing.

So when you really boil it down, empowering your employees is a brilliant way to induce engagement and bring out the best from everyone throughout the organization.

The problem isn't the idea of empowerment. Like so many other great leadership and business ideas, the problem is in the execution.

I'm pretty sure this is how empowerment (and other business advice) is rolled out in far too many organizations:

A manager surfs over to Harvard Business Review and they read an article about empowerment or attend a conference where a great motivational speaker says, "You have to empower your team to drive great results."

With a microphone in hand and a great lighting technician backstage, the speaker convinces the manager that angels are singing a song of empowerment. The answers to all of the manager's problems have been delivered (angels sold separately).

On Monday, when the manager heads back to the office he sits in his office and transforms into "The Empowerer" (Say it with a Schwarzenager accent for full effect). With this new training, the invigorated manager starts talking up and down the ladder about empowering the team and getting everyone involved. The new mantra is: a commitment to turn over a new leaf and to quit micro-managing things.

Yet, nothing is discussed as to how prepared the employees are for this transition.

Expectation setting, vision sharing, and highly engaged leadership are often left out of an empowered environment. Inspiration is great, but what about a plan for how the employees will really understand what they are empowered to decide? Has there been any internal analysis to determine whether the current team is ready or capable to take on the additional responsibility?

Really, empowerment is often just a line of well-intended business book jargon that is missing any real execution.

Picture this: the first employee that comes into the inspired manager's office and asks a routine question. The manager, with their new found "EmPOWERment Trip", says:

"What do you think you should do?"

The employee that is used to being given direction is stunned, lost and probably confused. Staring back like a deer into headlights, the employee is uncertain how to respond.

Then one of three things happens:

- The employee proceeds to do what she thinks she should, and messes it up

- The employee proceeds to do what she thinks, and happens to get it right

- The employee ends up reminding you that she asked you what to do because she doesn't know the answer.

If you get started at number 2, then everyone wins for now (because there is a good chance the employee got lucky).

If you get 1 or 3, then you are going to be frustrated, disenchanted and annoyed with your employee. Possibly, your annoyance will extend to the entire idea of empowerment because you have now grown convinced it doesn't work.

Of course, one incident - regardless of the answer - isn't going to validate anything. However, hopefully you get the gist.

Bottom line here is empowering the team is a strategy that must be incorporated with a number of other consistent leadership activities. Most importantly, new initiatives require messaging and expectation setting. Then, follow up with feedback and guidance so the empowered employee becomes better.

What I can tell you for sure is that telling your employee

to essentially "figure it out for yourself" is NOT empowerment. Nor is just throwing questions back at your team members.

The employee that is thrown into the fire will rarely come out alive let alone unscathed. How is trial by fire empowering? And, why do you think leadership even exists, if you expect your team to "figure it out" on their own?

To empower without active leadership support is really just an isolation exercise.

So yes, empower away. Give the employees the opportunity to thrive. But set them up to win.

Words are only words until they are given meaning. The leader is the one who makes victory possible. So there... now YOU are empowered to empower.

FOUR WAYS TO KEEP EMPLOYEES MOTIVATED AND ENGAGED

Tweet This:

Engaged employees are productive employees. How do you continually get the most from your teams?

Most leaders will tell you that hiring is a tricky science, if indeed it can be called a science at all.

With every new hire made, you want to believe that your latest decision is going to drive great results.

After all, you made the hire to improve your business. You aspire to see your instincts pay off, right?

What if I said that hiring in itself isn't the hard part? Rather, making great hires that are going to be long term contributors to the needs of the organization is the real challenge.

Any new hire you make is going to come in anxious to make a mark. Wanting to prove to new management and colleagues that they deserve to be there is what I call the universal "Fast Start." This Fast Start is the take-charge attitude that you see when a new hire is made, or a current employee is moved up within the organization.

I see the "Fast Start" behavior fizzle after a short period of time. Perhaps it is just human nature. The Fast Start and then the Fast Fizzle can be recognized across many facets of our lives, beyond the workplace.

For example:

- **Diet and Exercise:** So many people commit to a new diet or exercise plan where they dive in and completely entrench themselves in it for a short period of time only to fall off as quickly as they started.

- **Not So Prized Possessions:** People long to own a certain home, car or piece of jewelry. After obtaining it they are on Cloud Nine, only to become increasingly indifferent over time.

- **Social Relationships:** Over time most people establish their closest circles of friends. However, it is quite common for people to enter into intense platonic, professional and romantic relationships only to see them end as quickly as they started.

People are fickle creatures, some more than others. I believe it is safe to say that we all have something in our life that we have gotten really involved in, really quickly, and then uninvolved just as fast.

From Fast Start to Fast Fizzle: the key to making great hires is less about the hire itself and more about how you keep the employee motivated.

Most small and medium sized businesses hire employees with a role and an outcome in mind. For instance, a leader seeks to hire a new sales representative to expand the business in a certain territory. Further, the leader assumes that the new rep will generate (*insert best guess percentage here*) growth in business.

Many times the sales growth that is sought is directly proportionate to the amount being invested in the person. Here's the crazy part: often there is no actual plan for how the desired result will be accomplished.

So, after you hire and onboard the new employee, you have a few traditions that your new hire must follow. A ride along with a more senior person, for example, and some marketing materials that explain your company's product and services. You tell your new team member to read the info and pay close attention on the ride along, because soon the rookie will need to be out making sales alone.

After a few weeks, the new sales rep is sent off, on their own, to "Make It Happen." Management then returns to the day-to-day, and the assumption is made that the new hire has been assimilated into the culture.

Does this example sound familiar to you, and to your organization? Probably so, and the common nature of the story make the problem hard to see. The problem lies with motivation.

The key to keeping employees motivated is twofold. First, recognizing that motivation is fickle – it comes and goes and can change often. Second, how do you apply action to this awareness in order to keep your teams as engaged and excited as possible?

Here are four things that any organization can do to continue to get the most from their employees.

- **Clear Vision:** Employees quickly become disenchanted when they don't feel a clear sense of direction for the organization. It is amazing how many business leaders I have met that can't spell out their company vision quickly and concisely. If you want your employees to buy off on your vision *you have to know what it is*. Make your message clear and speak to it often, because many employees need the constant clarity to keep moving forward.

- **Train and Educate:** Do you ever feel you have reached the point where you know all that there is to know about your job? The answer is no. Even if you did know today everything that there is to know, things change so fast that by tomorrow you would be steps behind. In organizations small and large, I find that continued employee development is an afterthought – or completely non-existent. As a leader, how will an afterthought keep your employees motivated? All living things need to be nourished continuously, if you want them to grow and prosper. Consider training as one way to provide sustained nourishment.

- **Engage:** Make time for your employees, and when you do make time, make it meaningful! Your people are the lifeblood of your business. The processes and procedures can and should take a backseat to your people. Many business leaders turn to their processes long before they look to their people, when trying to lead growth and change in their business. Reverse this process, and start with people first.

- **Repeat, Repeat, Repeat:** The cycle of investing in the relationship and development of your team NEVER ends. Relationships can't be looked at as if once your initial connection is completed, then a box can be checked. Vision will change, education will never stop, and you must consistently make time for your people. Leadership is a process, and repetition is central to reputation. Duplicate your success, over and over again, and watch your influence grow.

I often speak about looking at processes after people. Not because processes aren't important, but because people come first. But here is a process that you can commit to:

Commit to providing your employees with the vision, development and personal relationship with the company that will keep them striving to drive great results. Commit to nurturing this relationship every day. And recognize that the relationship part of the job is never over.

If you want to stop the Fast Fizzle, then make sure to capture the essence of what excited your new hire in the first place! Commit to delivering that excitement, starting with your own passion for the business.

FOUR WAYS TO KEEP EMPLOYEES MOTIVATED AND ENGAGED

For your operation to succeed, you have to dedicate yourself to repeated doses of excellence – and that excellence has to be contagious. There are many ways to influence culture, and to keep employees engaged and enthusiastic, but all of these leadership strategies start at the same place.

Leadership starts with YOU.

AN AFTERWORD
ARE YOU READY FOR THE CORNER OFFICE?

Now that you have had the chance to share in my journey, I want to pose a question to you.

Are you ready for what's next?

For me, "next" was every success and every failure that brought me closer to my goals. "Next" was leading sales for a territory, then operations for a region and eventually, leading an entire company. And guess what, I believe there is so much more to still accomplish!

For you, "next" is whatever drives you towards your success. Failure isn't an outcome, it's a teacher. Learn from your mistakes. For me, I've learned that success is going to be based on three things.

1. How will you Lead?

2. How will you leverage Resources and Technology?

3. How will you Execute?

These three questions are not mutually exclusive. You've got to have every aspect covered, if you want to be a true leader today.

Lastly, and perhaps above all else: recognize that you are in control. Too often, we allow the external environment to assume control of what we as individuals are able to accomplish. Don't let your environment control you. Every day when we awake we have the opportunity to get behind the wheel of life. And you get to decide exactly how hard to press the gas and when to stomp the brake.

When this amazing journey began, I felt like I had been dropped inside of a traffic jam with no end in sight. And while you may not have the power to clear the road, you absolutely have the power to decide how you will respond and how you will make the most of your situation.

So lead courageously – and don't let life's traffic patterns get you off your path.

I like to remember what one of my great mentors told me:

> *"You haven't truly failed until you decide to stop trying."*

The corner office is yours for the taking.

I look forward to seeing you there!

ACKNOWLEDGEMENTS

This book never would have been possible without the guidance and input from my dear friend, colleague and pitch man extraordinaire Chris Westfall. His guidance and creativity made it possible for me to share the stories and experiences that comprise this book. To my wife Lisa, and my daughters Hailey and Avery who motivate me to reach for the stars every single day. They have been the foundation on which I have built my career. For that I cannot thank them enough, but I will continue to try! There are so many others through professional and personal accomplishments that deserve thanks. And while I cannot possibly put everyone individually here on this page (I could, but I won't) I hope you all know who you are and how much you mean to me. Finally, to my parents. Dad, you have been an inspiration to me. I still remember the day that I told you I never wanted to work hard like you when I grew up. I'm so glad you have had the chance to be a part of my professional and personal life. Your guidance is always appreciated. And Mom, your unconditional love and adoration has meant the world to me. Although I don't say it enough. Thank you.

If anyone had asked me 10 years ago if by my 31st birthday if I would have a story to tell that would be worth publishing, I probably wouldn't have believed them.

It is for this exact reason that I wrote this book. Whether you are 18 or 55, the opportunity to create a great story still exists. I can't wait to hear yours!